SYMBIOSIS

Nancy Tremaine

With

Michael Austin Melton, M.S., Psy.D.

And

David W. Chace

Printed in the United States of America

First Printing, August 2017

ISBN-13:   9781976250224
ISBN-10:   1976250226

Itsallconnected Publishing
445 Hudson Street
Winnipeg, Manitoba
Canada R3T OR1

tremaine.nancy@gmail.com

Table of Contents

Dedication

To my beautiful daughter, Stacy Michelle. I nicknamed her Peabody when she was a baby after Mr. Peabody, the cartoon character. Mr. Peabody was the smartest being in existence. I thought my daughter was the smartest child in the world. Stacy was extremely precocious. Only children have a tendency to grow up quickly, especially when they feel responsible for and feel they have to protect and take care of their mother. It's quite a responsibility to put on a child. For all the mistakes I made as a mother I ask for your forgiveness. I love you Stacy.

Acknowledgments

I wish to thank the following people for sharing, contributing or being a part of my journey.

Chuck Schingeck, Mr., Skinny Bob, The Reptilians, Cynthia Lutes Vandergriff, Fred Lutes, Doug Vandergriff, Chief Lee BeGole, Officer Martin Cone, David Ames, Dr. Harry Willnus, Vaughn Vowels, Nick Marroni, Landi Mellas, Joe Stewart, Patty Donahue, Hilary Porter, Roy Muck, Dr. John Mack, Chris Canton, Tom Beck, Barbara Morrell, Denise and Jack Koos, Erica Goetsch, Bridget Smith, Miesha Johnson, and Kathy Braun. Christine and Victor Hansen.

I wish to especially thank Dr. Harry Willnus and Vaughn Vowels who together made this journey for me possible. To my girlfriend Cindy and former Novi Police Chief Lee BeGole for being brave enough to share their memories, and to my cousins Chris Canton and Barbara Morrell who were the only family members I had throughout this journey.

Special thanks to Lonnie Huhman with The Novi News, Michael Austin Melton and Julia Weiss with Starborn Support Radio, Jason McClellan and Maureen Elsberry with Open Minds Magazine and Spacing Out, Ken Parsons with BEAMS Investigations, and Joanne Summerscales with AMMACH for giving me the opportunity to share my story with others.

I wish to thank the following people that took me under their wing and made this book possible: Grant Cameron, David Chace, Desta Barnabe, Doug Auld, Matt Lacasse and Katarina Castillo.

Foreword

Vaughn Vowels was and is a supporter of Nancy Tremaine from the very first day he entered her life and vicariously journeyed with her through her trauma and triumph. He wrote this letter in support of Nancy:

> As I sit down to tell my part of Nancy's story I can't help but reflect on the synchronistic change of events that brought us together. For Nancy, it all started in the summer of 1961 when she and her girlfriend Cindy encountered a silver disc shaped craft hovering near their homes in Novi, Michigan. Its red, white, and green lights changed their minds' landscape forever. I guess my journey toward acceptance of things that lay outside of the scientific, religious and educational establishments began in the December of 1967. That's when my world was turned upside down; it wasn't a close encounter, but rather the loss of my father at the age of 38. It was from this experience of utter devastation that a quest for knowledge and openness to all possibilities was born. My investment in this Earth plane being the "be all" and "end all" was shattered.
>
> In August of 2011 I ran into one of my fellow professors, Richard Thornes, Ph.D., in the Social Sciences Office at Lansing Community College. Richard and I had been teaching Adjuncts for nearly 15 years in the Psychology Department. Richard was also a working full-time Psychologist in the Lansing area. I had recently left a career of 22 years as an Outreach Family Therapist (Social Worker) in the Mid-Michigan area, and was fortunate to be given 4 class sections to teach that fall. Adjuncts rarely have the luxury of getting to know one another in any depth, because of the busy schedules we must keep to make up for the lack of compensation. Teaching for an Adjunct is a labor of love, or a waste of a student's time. On that fateful day in August we discovered that both of us had been trained as hypnotherapists by the same mentor (Robert Ranger), at the Institute for Transformational Therapy. As we shared stories of some of our hypnotic sessions, Richard

mentioned that he had been working with MUFON (the Mutual UFO Network) doing regressions, and that he was worried that his association with the organization might cause problems with his standing in the Psychiatric community. The possibility of losing his full-time job was weighing on his mind. When I mentioned that I hadn't any reservations about working with MUFON as a regression therapist, Richard gave me the phone number of Harry Willnus, Ed. D., the former director of Michigan's MUFON chapter. It was through Harry that I met Nancy on a pleasant fall day (September 11th, 2011) at his home in South Lyon, Michigan. It was the first time I'd ever met Harry. We sat on his back porch and got to know each other a bit. After about an hour I mentioned that I had been a head baseball coach at the college level. He asked me a series of questions about the game that my answers seemed to satisfy his belief in my character. Shortly thereafter he was on the phone with Nancy telling her that he felt comfortable that I was legitimate and could do the regressions she desired. Forty-five minutes later she pulled into the driveway and made her way up the stairs connected to the back porch.

Nancy stands about 5' 3" and can't weigh much more than one hundred pounds. She was 62 when I met her that day, but I had to say that her presence exuded sensuality. She was nervous, but articulate, obviously intelligent, and quite anxious about the possibility that hypnosis might release a flood of memories that she had only recently begun to process. It had been 50 years since her experience in Novi, Michigan and she wasn't completely convinced it was real. She described a variety of post-traumatic stress symptoms that were plaguing her life. These symptoms included panic attacks, depression, isolation, intruding obsessive thoughts, and fear of losing her sanity. I told her I didn't know what to believe as far as the alien presence on Earth, but that I believed her mind held the answers to her recovery and there must have been a part of her that wanted to heal. As a former Social Worker I knew that my 'rescue fantasies' could be put to the test that I'd partially left the field to avoid. But, I was all in. We set up a time to do the

4

first regression at Harry's sister's home on September 29th, 2011. Harry was present for all the regressions that we did between the dates of September 29th, 2011 and May 18th, 2012.

Introduction

My very first memories were of my father. I remember when I was very young tugging on his pant leg so he would pick me up. I remember his rough whiskers upon my face, and I remember his scent. I remember always feeling safe and secure in his arms. I was daddy's favorite, and it was never a secret to my other siblings. My dad was serving in World War II when my older sister was born, so he really did not get to know her until she was about three years old. I was the only baby girl. My dad's friends thought I'd never learn to walk because he never put me down.

My relationship with my mother was entirely different. We were never close. I was the third of five children – right in the middle, and I always felt like that baby bird in the nest that mother did not want. I became a pleaser and tried so very hard to get her attention and her love. She once told me there was no law that said a mother had to love her child. What a terrible thing to say to a little girl! I would often play the "what if" game with her. I would say, "What if you had to choose one of us kids to die, who would you pick?" Questions like this were probably just as cruel to a mother! She would always say something like, "What a horrible question that was! Why would you ask such a question?" I would say to myself, "I know it would be me…"

The first few months after I was born my mother went to work, and I was left in the care of my Aunt Jeannie. My aunt had just given birth to my cousin, so she breast-fed both of us at the same time. She would tell me she gave me "chocolate milk." I remember always wishing that Aunt Jeannie was my mother.

My mother and Aunt Jeannie were complete opposites. My mother was a prude and extremely modest. She never smoked, she never drank, and she never used curse words. My father was the only man she had ever been with. Everything was "crude" to my mother.

Aunt Jeannie was a partier! She preferred her men young. When she was in her seventies she was dating men who were in their twenties! She usually had a drink in one hand and a cigarette in the other. She was an absolute social butterfly and everyone loved her. She was quite popular wherever she went. People would drive for miles and miles just to drive by her house in hopes that the living room curtains might be open so they could catch a glimpse of the large black panther painted with green glow in the dark eyes that covered the entire wall. She wore as many gold chains as Mr. T, and her

6

fingernails and toenails were always polished gold. She had breast implants before most of the world even knew they existed, and she proudly showed off the tattoo on her back depicting a lightning bolt with the words "Born to Shock." In addition to this, she was a very generous, kind and loving woman and was ready to help anyone who needed it. I believe Aunt Jeannie loved me as much as she loved her own children, and I loved her as much as any daughter could love her mother.

My parents grew up three houses apart, and my dad's first love was my mother. He told his mother that when he grew up he was going to marry that little black haired girl, and he certainly did! He loved my mother from the age of nine until he died just before he turned eighty years old. Our home was filled with music, and my parents would often be seen dancing across the living room floor. They truly loved each other. My older brother and I practiced dancing together, and both of us could completely clear any dance floor. We were very good. To this day I still love to dance; I am a Motown girl!

The family operation consisted of routines. Everything we did was a routine. Our home was always spotless and everything was in perfect order. Dinner was always served shortly after six o'clock, because that is when dad got home from work. Sometimes I would ask, "What animal are we eating?" I can remember pushing the meat around on my plate and thinking how horrible I was, eating this poor cow or pig. I have not eaten red meat in over 20 years. After dinner my older brother and I would do the dishes. We would take turns washing and drying. Bedtime was nine o'clock at night, and we were met with the loud clap of my father's hands followed by the words, "Brush your teeth and tinkle! It's time for bed!" Like little soldiers we lined up for the bathroom, and afterwards, we were all tucked in bed. My parents had no idea how quickly I could open the window, pop the screen open and sneak out at night. My girlfriends would also sneak out of their houses. There were woods close to my house, and my girlfriends and I would meet up with boys to "make out..."

In my family we have one of those perverted uncles. This uncle molested several nieces and nephews, and at least one of his own children as well. What makes this situation even more disturbing – many of my family are aware of his behavior, and they still allow him in their lives and around their children. My family seems to be split in two: The half that have totally removed this molester and any family members associated with him from their lives, and the other half that refuse to believe it's true and continue to live in denial.

I have always preferred the company of animals to people. One of my brothers and I found a stray dog. He was nothing more than skin and bone and his eyes were infected. He had obviously been abused. We asked my dad for change so we could buy this poor mongrel, quite obviously part beagle, a can of dog food. My dad took one look at him and brought him inside. He was bathed, and his infected eyes were tended to. My dad called him Mitch, and told us we had a brother. Mitch lived for nearly twenty years and was truly a part of the family.

If someone were to describe me, they would surely say that I am overly emotional and extremely sensitive. I still cry at old Lassie episodes. Once, when my daughter was about four or five years old she was sitting on the sidewalk killing ants. I said to her, "What are you doing? Don't you realize that ants have families, too? You might have killed one of the ant's brothers or their mother!" I went on to explain how ants work together to carry food and take care of one another. Little did I know what an impression this made on her. Not so many years ago I heard her telling my grandson the exact words I had told her.

I was very popular in school as were all five of us kids. I was a track star, winning a trophy and three gold medals. I was also a cheerleader. I hated school with a passion and skipped classes every chance I got. I never understood why we had to learn things we would never use as adults. I also hated homework, but was smart enough to write a book report on the bus in the few minutes it took to get to school. None of us kids were allowed to get below a "C" because that would make us below average, and my parents refused to have a child that was below average. If I received a "C minus" I was grounded until the next marking period. On every report card I received the teachers would comment, "Nancy talks too much in class."

After my experience during the summer of 1961 I returned to school a different person. I would be held back that year. I remember being an angry child filled with rage. I often wonder how I would have turned out if my parents allowed me to talk about that day. Being held back destroyed my relationship with Suzie, my best friend from the first through seventh grade. We spent every minute we could together. We were the smallest girls in the class and the last to develop. The boys teased us for being so small.

My father's strict rules caused my older sister to leave home and live with our grandparents. My older brother did the same. There were only my two younger brothers and me left living at home. My parents purchased a camper with a bathroom and a small kitchen so we could travel during the summers, and they tried to take us to every state.

We even went to the 1964 World's Fair in New York City. Most of my time in the car was spent writing love letters to the two boyfriends I had from the age of thirteen until I was seventeen. My mother would say, "Pay attention, because someday you are going to marry a man that never takes you anywhere." There was a lot of fighting and bickering between my two brothers and me, and my dad would reach around and smack all three of us at once. We would all wind up in tears, and mom would say to dad, "Now look what you've done!"

I ended up getting pregnant at seventeen, and it was not from either of my two boyfriends. It was from an older guy I was set up with. He had a red convertible Thunderbird and bought me expensive gifts. After the third morning of missing school and puking my guts out my, mother asked me if I was pregnant. I told her no, because we didn't "do it" all the way.

I was promptly taken to the doctors where my mother would be told that he could not examine me because I had an intact hymen. I said to her, "See, I told you, mom!" Yes, I was pregnant, and technically still a virgin. Apparently, the first inch counts. My daughter swims like a fish and often jokes that she was a good swimmer back then as well.

My father suffered several heart attacks. The first one was shortly after I got pregnant. My mother told me if my dad died I would have to live with the guilt. That was some pretty heavy shit to put on a teenage girl. I believed his heart attack was my fault for years after.

When I told my daughter's father I was pregnant, he asked me what I wanted him to do about it. I said through tears and innocence, "Well, I think you are supposed to marry me." He fired back at me, "I ain't marrying you!" However, his mother had other plans for him: He could marry me, or he could go to prison for statutory rape. Well, he chose marriage over jail.

We went to a Justice of the Peace, and it was done in minutes. When we got to the parking lot, I told (the guy's name was) Bill to look me in the eyes, and I said these words, "Let's promise to always stay married and love each other forever." His reply was, "Yeah, yeah, yeah, now get in the fucking car." We drove to a furnished upper flat

9

that he had rented for us and he dropped me off where I was left alone with all of my stuffed animals. He didn't come home at all that night.

I sat on the bed striking a pose waiting for him. He never touched me again. He told me I made him sick. He hated me for getting pregnant. My mother stopped by and presented me with a bucket and mop and cleaning supplies. She dropped them off and said, "Welcome to married life."

At seventeen, having a baby without the love of the child's father or the support of your parents is very difficult. My father refused to talk to me during my entire pregnancy. My mother told me it was because he was too ashamed to look at me.

It was July 29th at nine o'clock in the evening, and my daughter's father and I were headed out to see a movie. As I reached for the gate, a flood came from below. I started to cry because I was embarrassed and said, "I wet my pants," He told me my water had broken. I had no idea what that meant, but it sounded really scary, and I called my mom. She told me to get to the hospital immediately. The hospital where I was scheduled to give birth was in downtown Detroit, and the riots of 1967 were in high gear, so I had to go to another hospital. St. Mary's hospital was a Catholic hospital – I am not a Catholic.

In 1967, being pregnant at seventeen automatically meant you were a "slut," and that is exactly how the nuns in residence treated me.

I was in the hospital for three hours and the labor pains hadn't started, so I was given a shot to induce labor. On top of that, my labor would be dry because my water had broken. The pain was so intense.

With each set of contractions I would lose consciousness. In retrospect, I realized I was way too tiny to give birth naturally because during the birthing process I could actually watch my hipbones spread apart! They refused to give me anything for the pain so I was forced to have a natural childbirth. No one was allowed in the room with you back then except for your husband, and frankly, he had no interest in being with me.

I cried out for my mother, and a nun got right in my face and mimicked me, "I want my mom, I want my mom. Well the next time you will know to keep your pants on, won't you?"

A beautiful black nurse came to my rescue. She forced the nun to one side and cradled me to her chest, saying to the nun, "She is just a baby, can't you see that?" I held on to her tightly as she ran a cool washcloth across my face. I begged her to stay with me and not leave me alone with the nuns.

Finally, at about five the next morning my daughter's head began crowning. I was whisked quickly into the delivery room; I was starting to give birth. A doctor pushed my baby's head back inside the birth canal. I was forced to sit up and hold my legs together tightly as they administered an epidural.

My daughter was born at 5:06 am! I waited for the "slap" on the butt, as the doctor held her upside down and she began to cry. I asked the nurses if I could hold her, but instead, they immediately placed her in an incubator.

In those days you did not get to hold your baby after giving birth. She was screaming and bright red with her hands balled up into little fists and her little legs curled up toward her stomach. I knew this process was the wrong approach.

I felt a mother should immediately hold their new baby. They then wheeled her out of the room, and it would be several hours before I would get to meet my own child.

Finally, a nurse emerged with my daughter and gently placed her on my breast. Her eyes were beautiful and blue, with a tuft of black hair at the nape of her neck which I named a ducktail. I thought to myself, "My mother will love this one." After all, my mother ordered all of her children to have black hair and blue eyes.

My mother named my daughter Stacy after some woman she had met, and who apparently was beautiful with black hair and blue eyes. The name is very appropriate. So, there I was, a young woman with a newborn child, with no education and no way to support myself. Tell me, what is a girl to do? Get a job!

My girlfriend found an advertisement seeking a "Go-Go Girl." It paid five bucks per hour plus tips. All dancers had agents back then.

I met with this agent doing the hiring. I was underage, and he knew it. Despite my age, he asked me to audition. The music started, and I passed out cold right there on the dance floor. He got me a drink once I came to, then I got up and I went back on stage, and "a star was born!"

I was making money hand over fist. It was not uncommon for me to bring home a couple hundred bucks just in tips, not counting my five dollars per hour salary, all under the table! That career lasted for a bit over a year until the "topless" fad came in.

I am ashamed to say I was a horrible mother. I was selfish, and resented being burdened with a baby. Every time she cried, I cried along with her. I just wanted to party, and that is what I did. I would give anything to undo those years and repair the pain I caused my daughter. I have tried so hard to make it up to her, but there would never be enough time. I know it breaks her heart when she watches me with the grandchildren wishing I could have been like that for her. She punished me for many years, and I allowed it because I felt I deserved it.

I met husband number two in a bar. Actually, he was the bartender and he had served in Vietnam, and had been discharged for a few years when I met him. He suffered from Post-Traumatic Stress Disorder and had a drug problem.

Our relationship became troubled over time, and we moved to Florida to try and save our marriage. Instead he wound up finding new friends with drugs.

I sent him packing to Michigan, and my daughter and I stayed in Florida for another six years. I met husband number three in a bar as well. We were seated next to each other and we started chatting.

He told me he was a marine biologist. I then asked him, "Oh! How long have you been in the Marine Corps?" After he realized I was asking him with all sincerity, he said to me, "I have never met anyone like you!" We danced for hours, and it was obvious he was crazy about me.

At the end of the evening, I drove the twenty-minute ride home. As I parked and exited the car, I noticed his car behind me on the roadway. He followed me home! I was quite alarmed at first, but then as he slowed down, he rolled his window down and shouted that he just wanted to make sure I got home safely.

After three days of dating I was greeted by him at the front door of my apartment with a big bouquet of flowers and proclaimed, "I can't eat, sleep, or do anything except think about you. You have to marry me!"

I laughed and said to him, "You don't even know me." He replied, "I know all I need to know. I have never felt like this!" Well, of course I said no, but he was insistent, and my family thought I should be flattered that a "Ph.D." marine biologist from a wealthy family wanted to marry me.

He was extremely handsome, classy, and well spoken, and I was proud of him and flattered that he was so taken by me. After three months I finally said "Yes," and he quickly drove me to Valdosta, Georgia where you can get married in one day. I had absolutely no idea what I had gotten myself into. He was the most intelligent man I had ever met.

He was also the most evil man I had ever met, a true sociopath. He was abusive, and I believe if I hadn't gotten out of the marriage when I did he would surely have murdered me. I know in my heart he would have. We divorced in 1980 and my daughter and I moved back to Michigan.

I remained single for ten years, and married husband number four in 1990 and divorced him three years later. I have been single now for twenty-two years, and I didn't date for several years. I never had a relationship last more than three years.

In 2004, my father's sister, Aunt Jewel, called me. It was the only time I can remember her calling me. Shortly after we spoke on the phone, she died. Out of nowhere she said to me, "I don't know why your mother never loved you. You were always a sweet, loving girl."

I cried not because I was sad, but because she loved me enough to tell me what I needed to hear. I thanked her because for the first time someone acknowledged what I had known all my life. I forgave my mother after all those years.

My family is a dysfunctional mess. Many of my family members are screwed up because of "that uncle" I cannot talk about. The uncle that took the kids camping, bought them gifts, and then molested them.

One of his victims overdosed on drugs a few months ago and died. My daughter is another one of his many victims. It is amazing how much damage one person can leave in his wake. Removing myself from much of the family has been an easy choice, and was basically the only choice I had.

One of the last conversations I remember having with my father was a brief period when my mother was not around, which was very infrequent. He was sitting in his recliner, and I asked him if I was too old to sit on his lap. He smiled and patted his thigh.

I sat on his lap and wrapped my arms around his neck. Then, pulling back, I looked him straight into his eyes and said, "Dad, I just want you to know that I love you more than any daughter has ever loved their father. We have been together in every life in the past, and we will always be together. Your death will not separate us."

I watched my father try to hold back the tears, but they filled his eyes despite his efforts. I am so glad I had this conversation with him. A lot of people regret not voicing their words. I told my dad that the only thing I wanted when he died was all of the love letters he wrote to my mother during World War II.

He reacted with surprise, and I realized no one else had ever mentioned them. A short time after that I was visiting my parents, and when my mother left the room my dad motioned me to follow him to the den and told me to open my car trunk. "Quickly," he said, "put these boxes in. These are the letters I wrote to your mother. Do not tell her I gave these to you, she would have a fit!" I could not wait to get home so I could read these letters! I have shoe boxes filled with three years of love letters.

Despite the trauma I went through, I think I came out of it pretty damn well. Before we leave this introduction however, I want to share a few things about myself that came to mind. It represents a few of my eccentricities and they will in a way round out who I am today.

In 2009, a part of me died when I had to have my cat, "Cuddle Bugs," put to sleep. She had been my best friend and constant companion for nearly nineteen years. I took her everywhere with me. She loved car rides and basket rides. Basket rides were done with a laundry basket and a long piece of twine tied on one end that would allow me to pull her through the apartment. She loved when I would run taking corners causing the basket to turn on its side. She would brace herself and ride out the sharp turns. Sometimes she would fly out, but was quick to jump back into the basket even if it was still in motion. We really communicated, and I am sure she understood everything I said. I would cradle her in my arms and we would stare into each other's eyes.

She even humored me by allowing me to dress her in her Santa outfit every Christmas, even though she disliked it. I would tell her how beautiful she was and how much I loved her. Near the end she had arthritis, and her bladder was failing. Even though she was in tremendous pain, she continued to jump off the bed and followed me into the bathroom in the middle of the night waiting while I peed. We were inseparable. The pain I felt after losing her caused my heart to ache and I thought I too would die. I couldn't imagine life without her, and I missed holding her and carrying her everywhere. So, I purchased a small stuffed black cat that looks very much like Cuddles. For the first year I carried this stuffed animal constantly and even took her in the car and for overnight visits. It never entered my mind how odd it looked to others. I still have her, and she sits next to me as I type these words.

I own a mannequin, and I named her Vanity. I got her about six years ago. I have two wigs for her, one blonde, and the other dark.

We wear the same size, so I dress her in my clothes. She stands in the corner of my dining room. A good friend of mine who passed several years ago had always told me to "...remember, this is your life and everyone else is just passing through." So I don't care what other people think about my being quirky. I rather enjoy it!

Chapter 1
Is This Real?

That is at bottom the only courage that is demanded of us: to have courage for the most strange, the most singular and the most inexplicable that we may encounter. That mankind has in this sense has been cowardly has done life endless harm; the experiences that are called "visions," the whole so-called "spirit-world," death, all those things that are so closely akin to us have by daily parrying been so crowded out of life that the senses with which we could have grasped them are atrophied. To say nothing of God. - Rainer Maria Rilke

It was the summer of 1961. I was twelve years old. My father had come home from work, so it had to be after six o'clock in the evening. He arrived home from work at precisely five after six every night. Normally, we kids would have been washing our hands and getting ready for dinner in the formal dining room, but not that night. My mother had taken a part-time job four days a week, from five to nine o'clock in the evening, at a small fruit and vegetable market a few miles from home. Mother certainly did not have to work; my father worked as a hydraulic engineer for Sperry Vickers Corporation in the aerospace division for over thirty years.

My father was strict, and very overprotective. Our lives were very regimented. He kept the five of us kids in line! Spankings were common and often. We were all well-mannered, always clean and well dressed. I remember more than once people referring to us as "little soldiers." Dad always carried a comb, a tube of ChapStick and a hankie. Every hair on our heads was always combed, and he was constantly putting ChapStick on our lips. If we had a smudge of dirt on us dad was quick to spit on his hankie and wipe away the stain. I spent much of my childhood grounded. I realize now that it was because he was relieved to know exactly where I was.

That evening, dad agreed to let me go to my friend Cindy's house and play. There was a direct view from our front door to hers. I was never allowed to go out past dusk, but it was summer, so it stayed light outside until about nine o'clock. Although it was a beautiful evening outside, we decided to play inside. Suddenly, Cindy's father was yelling for us to come outside, with urgency and excitement in his voice. As we walk out the front door, we were met with the sight of a shimmering silver ship hovering above a fully leafed oak tree that stood between her house and mine. I can only compare the moment we walked out her front door to the scene in "The Wizard of Oz" where the movie went from black and white to brilliant color. There was no sound; it was completely silent. The lights on the ship were red, green, and white, and I couldn't tell if they were rotating or pulsating. They were moving so fast, I could not tell. I didn't feel fear, just awe and excitement that I was fortunate enough to be seeing this. The only name I could think to put to it was "flying saucer!" It was enormous! It was at least as large as my ranch home, and twice as tall. I do not recall any sound coming from the ship or from any of us gathered around. Cindy's father was adjusting the lens of a telescope and asked us if we would like to look through the lens. I could not believe he would ask such a thing! I mean, there it was, right in front of us. I did not want to take my eyes off of it for one single second. I willed it to stay there. I wanted everyone to see what I was seeing; I wanted this to last forever. Even though it was early evening, the sky was blue and cloudless. The sight was beautiful, and breathtaking!

A police car pulled up to where we were all standing. Two officers exited the car, and I was thrilled that they also were able to see this. I can only imagine what they must have been thinking. I remember tugging at one officer's arm as I struggled to voice three simple words. My voice deepened and decelerated. I was now in slow motion as I asked the question, "Is……. this……. real?" I had to be sure this was really happening. I wanted to make sure that what I was witnessing was also being witnessed by others. How does a child process such an overload of visual stimulation? The officer never answered me. He only glanced down at me and then quickly returned his gaze to the ship. We were all shocked at what we saw next. A car was coming down Meadowbrook Road, the street where my home was located. We knew the people in the car were seeing what we were seeing, but the car continued to drive toward us as it slowly approached the ship. I wondered to myself who was driving that car and what they must have been thinking. Fifty years later I would learn that it was an off-duty Novi, Michigan police officer named Martin Cone. He was in an unmarked patrol car and was patrolling a nearby area under construction. I would also learn that he had called Chief Lee BeGole, who was on duty in the Novi police station a few miles away, and reported a "Strange object overhead." What happened next is when the event went from awe to fear. A bright light emerged from the bottom of the ship, and it was directed at the unmarked car. The

17

light slowly worked its way down to the hood of the approaching car. I was very curious what this beam of light would do when it reached the car. Finally the beam made contact with the hood of the car, and the car stopped dead in its tracks! I instinctively knew that the beam of light had immobilized and disabled the car.

At that point I began doing jumping jack motions and yelled to the ship "Over here, over here!" I thought I might be trying to distract the ship from harming whoever was in the car. I honestly never figured out what possessed me to do that. I do remember that it infuriated Cindy who grabbed my arms and tried to quiet me. The ship then tilted on its side to acknowledge my presence, and I clearly remember receiving the message "We see you," I remember feeling almost hysterical, and I approached the uniformed officer again and tugged on his arm. I shouted, "Do something!" He was a police officer after all, and he had a gun, and he was supposed to protect us. He did nothing. I had never seen fear in a man's face before, and I realized we were all helpless. This was a defining moment. I thought I would never again feel safe and protected in this world. Everything I had known and believed was forever changed. At this point I experienced missing time. It was getting dark now. I didn't understand or even try to make sense of it.

My very next memory was of being at home with my father. I remember calling my mom at work and excitedly telling her what we had seen. She seemed so calm, and told me she heard about it from several customers that came into the store. I couldn't understand then, and I still don't understand why she didn't come home immediately. Why couldn't she understand how much I needed her? She told me she was getting off work shortly, so I knew it was just before nine o'clock in the evening. She would be home at ten minutes after nine o'clock as she always was. I was bursting to share.

I remember my father trying to assure me that I was home and I was safe. That night I was silenced. Before telling me never to speak of this event again my father shared some private information with me, and it was never to be shared with my mother. I believe this conversation with my father, which is relayed farther along in this book, is what bonded us to form the close relationship we had.

Bedtime for me was nine o'clock at night, but I remember my parents let me stay up late that evening. I remember that I couldn't sleep that night, and that I spent a very long time standing on the headboard of my bed so I could see out of the window. I wanted to see the oak tree that only a short time earlier had that ship hovering

18

above it. As I gazed out of my bedroom window that night, and many nights after, I repeated over and over again, "Please come back and get me, come back and get me!"

I do not remember the next day or the events of the previous evening ever being mentioned by my parents or by me. I just knew I had a secret, and I couldn't tell anyone! I tried the best I could to store these memories in a private place in my mind where no one could get to them. It was simply never spoken about again, not even with Cindy. Cindy and I started seventh grade in the fall, and I made new friends. We quickly grew apart, and as we got older Cindy's drinking would always be the reason I would distance myself from her. Over the course of the next 50 years the incident was never mentioned again, not to a boyfriend, husband, or even therapist. There were those frustrating moments when someone would joke about little green men or flying saucers, and I would bite my tongue as the anger grew inside me. Every year or so I would draw a picture of the ship and the car it immobilized, and I would show it to my daughter. After several years she was very disinterested, so I would draw it for my own sanity and afterward, I would quickly discard it.

Cindy would enter my life every few years. I would try to get her to open up, but she would become aggravated and fearful. I begged her one time to "please" tell me that it happened. She finally said "It happened, and I do not want to talk about it!" Cindy and my disinterested daughter were all I had. I had no one else for support. I tried to put that event out of my mind; I wanted it to just go away. I feel it is important here to reveal that I have never watched "Star Wars," "Lost in Space," or any of those phony shows. After all, I saw the real thing, and I didn't want to see jokes and fantasy made of something I knew was real. To this day, I read only biographies or autobiographies. I am only interested in true stories. I know the reality, and I could never settle for fiction.

My life was forever filled with anxiety, fear of doctors, especially needles, panic attacks, post-traumatic stress, and rage. I went to several therapists over the years, but never mentioned that day back in 1961. What I told them was that I knew there was something inside me that needed to come out. I explained to the therapists that I would get this burning sensation or smell in my nose every year or two, and that I knew there were memories attached to this. I begged every therapist to hypnotize me so I could remember what it was. They all told me in one form or another that they either didn't believe in hypnosis, or didn't think it would help me at all. Each therapist

19

assigned a different diagnosis to my anxiety and panic attacks. They all wanted me to try whatever new medication they were trying to push. Fifty years later, and after three regressions, I would come to know what that burning sensation with the memories attached was: ozone, electricity or electromagnetism of some sort.

The Ship Immobilizing the Police Car

Cindy pulling my arm down. I am yelling, "Over here! Over here!"

Chapter 2
Healing Begins When Someone Bears Witness

Healing begins when someone bears witness, and for me that meant meeting Dr. Harry Willnus. Up until the first day of September 2011 I had thought of myself as scar tissue. I actually voiced those words when I tried to describe how I felt about myself.

I found Dr. Willnus on the Internet. I never knew there was such a person as a ufologist. At that time, I wasn't even sure anyone really researched this phenomenon. Dr. Willnus had been following the subject of UFOs for over 55 years, and he was a former Michigan state director for MUFON. He has written several articles on the subject, and told me he was one of the investigators who worked on the alleged "swamp gas" event involving Dr. J. Allen Hynek.

I sent Dr. Willnus an email telling him that I had a story he might find interesting involving a UFO I had seen as a child. He wasted no time in calling me; he called me that same day. In turn, I wasted no time pouring my heart out to him, telling him everything I had held inside of me for half of a century. That moment had a great impact on me. I consider that day my very first day of healing. It was the first day of me learning to love me! Thank you, Harry.

A few days after that phone call we decided to meet at a restaurant. Harry came armed with lots of books and pictures of aliens. I looked at the pictures of these strange aliens, and not one of them stirred me emotionally. Those pictures had little or no effect on me.

Harry then asked if I could draw a picture of the UFO I had seen. I laughed and said, "Are you kidding? I can draw that picture in three minutes along with the car, the police and the houses!" And that I did! Harry was quite impressed. It was wonderful to finally have someone who wanted to see my drawing, and actually showed interest in it. I felt comfortable sharing my experiences, as I knew he believed me and didn't think I was crazy or delusional.

I told him of my intense fear of doctors and needles, and told him about my post-traumatic stress and anxiety. I told him about the burning smell that had come to me over the years and how it was attached to my memories. I told him I wanted to remember that day more clearly, and I wanted to know why my last memory was of the immobilized car, and I wanted to know how I got home that evening.

On September 8, 2011, just one week after meeting Willnus, I received an email from him telling me that he had found a possible regression therapist. He said he was working on setting up a time to meet with him because he had a lot of questions for him.

Willnus advised that we proceed with caution. He said that he would not allow just anyone to do the regression procedure without both of us feeling comfortable with him. Dr. Willnus' main concern was that the procedure might do more harm than good. He was also concerned about an experience I had had with a gynecologist who had molested me when I was seventeen years old. Harry offered to be with me during the regression if that would make me feel more comfortable.

On September 10, 2011, Willnus sent me another email telling me that he had spoken with the regression therapist, a Mr. Vaughn Vowels, and that he had a positive feeling about him. He told me that if I felt comfortable with the situation, I was welcomed to show up the next day at his house and meet Dr. Vowels. The next day, September 11th, I would meet Vaughn Vowels, the man who would potentially be my regression therapist.

On my way to Harry's house I had to stop and get gas, and of course something would happen to alter my neatly laid plans. There was a kitten amongst the gas pumps and it was crying and running up to people as if to say "please help me!"

I love cats and they have always been my favorite animal, and I have never been able to turn away from a stray. Today, however, I just didn't want or need the hassle. I picked up the kitten and pleaded with some guy to take it, but he refused. I took the kitten and placed it safely under a bush off to the side of the gas station.

The kitten, of course, stood there bewildered! It was a pitiful sight so I picked her up and placed her on the passenger seat of my car. She was crying and meowing, just making me miserable. I wondered if she might be hungry or thirsty, and I knew I didn't have time to stop because I was running behind.

My heart was racing, and I wondered how I was going to make this thirty-minute drive. The entire way, my focus was on this pitiful helpless animal. My constant and faithful companion of nearly nineteen years, "Cuddle Bugs," had just been put down, and I adamantly refused the idea of another pet and heartbreak. After passing Dr. Willnus' house a few times, I decided to call him. "I can't find your house, and I have this kitten in my car that I found at the gas station and it's crying and I don't know what to do with it!"

23

I was close to a panic attack, and I must have sounded like a crazy lady! Harry tried to calm me down and told me everything would be okay. I finally pulled into his long driveway and parked my car. I was greeted by a big, black beautiful dog called "Venus." I was afraid to open the car door for fear that Venus would jump into the car and hurt or possibly kill this little kitten.

Finally, Harry called Venus to him and I exited the car, leaving the passenger window open just enough for the kitten to get fresh air. I could only hope she would not use my car as a litter box!

As I walked toward the porch where the two men were seated, I thought to myself that they must think I am crazy, calling them, lost and panicking because of a silly stray kitten.

I was shaken and extremely rattled. I wondered if this regression therapist had already made up his mind and was going to leave. I tried to act cool, and slowly pulled myself together. I realized that I would never get this opportunity again, so I abandoned any and all fears I had about the kitten.

I locked eyes with Vaughn Vowels as I reached out to shake his hand. Dr. Vowels' laid back attitude put me at ease; he was almost shy, and seemed sweet. I trusted him right away and was grateful that he had made the long drive to meet with us. I showed him the illustrations I had taken with me. I recall having two of them.

Vaughn had very limited knowledge of UFOs and alien abductions, but he had done over 400 past-life regressions. Vaughn has a Bachelor of Arts degree from Michigan State University and a Master of Science degree from West Georgia University. He graduated with a 4.0 average in 1985. He spent seven years as a team, group and family counselor at a residential juvenile delinquency facility in Albion, Michigan. Now, after a couple of hours of very comfortable conversation, we all agreed to set a date to proceed with my first regression.

The regression took place at Harry's sister's house on September 29, 2011. Things were moving fast, to my satisfaction. In the month of September alone, I met Dr. Willnus, Vaughn Vowels, and was having my first regression. That evening it was rainy, miserable, and I had a very hard time finding the house, so I again called Harry. After pulling up to the house, as I ran up to the house in the pouring rain holding my umbrella, I was greeted by Harry and his sister. I was shaking and very emotional, and I'm not sure if it was from the chill or the anticipation, or perhaps a measure of both.

24

Harry's sister was very calm, and her soft, smooth voice had a comforting effect on me. I removed my coat and shoes and was then escorted to a room situated right off the dining room where Vaughn was seated, waiting for me.

Harry's sister closed the door behind us as I positioned myself on the couch, with Harry seated in a chair to my right, and Vaughn seated in a chair to my left. I was struggling, trying to remove a coin bracelet I was wearing, and I cut myself – the clasp had cut into my skin. I noticed a trickle of blood running down my arm.

"Oh, my God," I said, "I am so sorry!" Harry jumped up and called his sister to the room to assess the damage. She quickly wrapped my arm in a towel, and then returned promptly with a proper bandage. My only concern was bleeding on her beautiful sofa. She couldn't have been kinder as she bandaged my arm and told me not to worry, and that it was okay. She instructed me to "…just relax."

I took a few deep breaths, and Vaughn asked me to get comfortable. I had seen on television that people lie down when they get hypnotized, so that is what I did.

I thought to myself, "I am not sure this is going to work." As I lay there on the couch, I recall reaching my right hand out to Harry for comfort. I considered him my protector – I saw him as a father figure. He gently grasped my hand, and I immediately relaxed. Vaughn started to speak.

I do not remember exactly what he said, but he had very soft music on in the background as he spoke very slowly. I don't remember much of that hour of regression, but the few minutes I do remember are very clear to me. I remember feeling paralyzed.

I fought to move my arms and my legs, and I was angry; there was nothing I could do about it. Then I recall Vaughn trying to pull me out of the trance. I found myself fighting his words. I was now in a state of euphoria. I knew I was being taken up into their ship.

My body was waving and rumbling to the low hum of the ship. That was the first time I had ever used the word "rumbling" as it had never been a part of my vocabulary. I clearly recall using those words, however.

I was experiencing a feeling of pure ecstasy. To this day I have never felt that sensation again, and I longed to feel it again. Before the euphoria of going up into the ship I was frantically running home. I knew they were going to get me and I knew they were going to do it with an electric shock in the middle of my back.

25

While I was running and screaming "Don't get me!" I was waiting for that shock. I knew it was coming!

When the shock finally hit me I was immediately paralyzed, and it reminded me of a cartoon where I was frozen into position – my arms and legs were still in the running position. I then found myself on my back as I was moving up toward the ship. I was in some form of energy wave and it felt wonderful. I did not realize at the time Vaughn was trying to pull me out of the trance I was in.

When I became aware of it I fought his attempts to bring me out of the trance because I wanted to stay in that euphoria. I kept repeating, "My body is waving and rumbling to the low hum of the ship."

Soon after, I was fully awake and I was left wondering what would have happened next if Vaughn had extended the session. After the session was completed, the three of us went out for a bite to eat, and to discuss the session.

I was now positive that there was more to this abduction event, and I was going to get to the bottom of it. I felt we became "The Three Musketeers." That moment was when my obsession with ufology kicked in. I began reading everything I could get my hands on.

Dr. Willnus armed us both with several books on the subject. I couldn't wait to get home and gobble up every word! I thought to myself, "It's real! It's really, really real!" I was now set on a journey full of questions I needed answers to. I became my own investigator, and four years on, I continue to search for answers. I am not the same person I was prior to this regression. I am different, but still need to grow. I am proud of the fact that I am now on my way to understanding what happened to me.

Getting hit with the Beam of Light

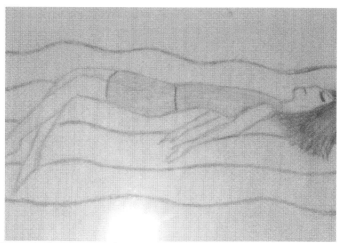

Nancy's body waving and rumbling as she is taken up

Chapter 3
The Investigation Begins

After that first regression I knew there was so much more to that first sighting than just seeing a UFO. I was determined to find out the whole story. It was vital to find witnesses who were present on that summer evening back in 1961. I felt it was crucial that I prove to Harry and Vaughn that I was not crazy and I was telling the truth.

In reality, it was more important to prove it to myself. My first thought was to contact friends on Facebook that were living in my neighborhood at that time. I found David; we lived about a block from each other, and he was on my "friends list." I sent him an email with my phone number, and asking him if he lived in Novi in 1961, and to please call me regarding a private matter. His call came on the 5th of October – the day after my sixty-second birthday. I told David about the UFO and what I recalled of that day.
He never balked or questioned my story; he believed me from the start. He told me that if I needed information regarding Novi to contact Lee BeGole, as he was the residing police chief at that time.

Google is the answer to everything! All I had to do was put "Novi, Michigan chief Lee BeGole," and the search found a page on the internet stating that the following day, October 6, 2011, Chief BeGole was to be honored by having a street named after him.

"What are the odds," I thought "the following day!" Again, what are the odds that after 50 years I would find the chief of police the day before his ceremony? Chief BeGole was still alive and 91 years old at that time. I realized time was fleeting for both of us, and I knew I had to be at that street naming ceremony. I quickly got to work on the following letter and placed it in an envelope to present to him the next day:

October 5th, 2011

Dear Chief BeGole;

My name is Nancy Schingeck Tremaine. I believe you knew my family. We moved to Novi in 1956 or 1957. My family lived on Meadowbrook Road located just off ten mile Road. I believe and hope you can answer some questions that have haunted me for many years.

28

There was a sighting of a craft (UFO) in Novi in the early sixties. The Novi Police arrived on Borchart Drive and joined in witnessing what we, Mr. Fred Lutes, his daughter Cindy, our neighbors and I were watching. I know there were others, but I don't know their names. The craft hovered silently above and to the right of a tree off of Meadowbrook Road and Mallot. The craft was silver and had colored strobe lights. There was no sound. There was an interaction between the craft and an oncoming car. My mother was at Hunt's Market while this occurred, and was aware of the event from several customers. I know that I spent much of the night staring out of my bedroom window waiting for it to return. I was encouraged not to talk about it because my parents hoped that I would forget. I never did talk about it, but I never forgot. It was always in the back of my mind. If I tried to mention it to Cindy, she would just walk away. Both she and her father kept it to themselves. There was no police report made which caused me and I am sure others to doubt their sanity.

This event has affected me for fifty years. I recently started to talk about this experience with a friend, and he has encouraged me to pursue it. I went to Facebook and contacted a school mate from Novi, David Ames. He said you were the chief officer at the time, and if anyone had the answers, it would be you.

I Googled your name, and to my amazement you will be in Novi tomorrow having a street named in your honor. Now, tell me this isn't a coincidence! Of course, I will be there to hand you this letter and pray you will call me so we can talk. Please call me.

Most sincerely,
Nancy Schingeck Tremaine

Chief BeGole holding Nancy's letter

I arrived early for the street signing the next day. I had the envelope in my hand and I was excitedly searching with my eyes for this man I hoped held answers I so desperately needed.

There he stood surrounded by people wanting to shake his hand and take a few minutes to speak with him. I wanted to scream, "Help me," but I waited for an opening and jumped in introducing myself and I handed him my "sacred" envelope.

He immediately began opening the letter, and I stopped him quickly and asked him to please open it later. For the next hour Chief BeGole held that letter in his hand. Only when he reached the podium to speak did he put my letter down. For the next several days I never let my phone out of my sight. I willed Chief BeGole to call me, but it didn't happen. I started questioning my sanity and myself once more.

On October 13, 2011, I had my second regression. It was one week to the day since handing the chief that important letter. The regression took place in my apartment and of course, Harry was there. The regression was recorded, and the following contains information derived from that session.

Please note that during these regressions "adult Nancy" is not always the one answering Vaughn; the "child Nancy" is present as well.

This has made it very difficult for me to listen to these regressions. It broke my heart to hear "little Nancy," as I refer to her, in fear and pain. Up until two years ago, I believed I was suffering with dissociative disorder, also known as "multiple personality disorder."

Most therapists I consulted told me it didn't exist. Only one therapist acknowledged it to be a real disorder, but added that it was not recognized as a disorder in the medical community, thus she could not address it in her diagnosis.

I had several different personas named Nancy that all had their purpose and function. Since the healing began over three years ago I have let some of them go because they are not needed anymore. My friends will attest to the fact that I'm not the same person (or persons) I was prior to starting this healing journey. Before a regression session, I made sure all phones were off – no interruptions! My journey was just too valuable. This was how every subsequent session began.

Once regressed, Vaughn asks me where I am and what I am doing. Little girl Nancy says, "I am jumping up and down, almost doing jumping jacks trying to get their attention! I am so excited – I want them to see me. Cindy thinks I am crazy." Vaughn said "But you are not crazy, are you?"

"No," I reply, "I am brave." My tone changes now and I say, "It sees us. I'm scared now. I know it's gonna get me. I want to hide, but there is no place to hide! They are gonna get me, they are gonna get me – and I can run fast. I'm hauling ass, don't get me… don't get me!" I am panting and my breathing is heavy from running.

After a pause, my voice goes monotone. "…They got me." I sounded defeated. I tell Vaughn "They are waiting for me inside." My voice raises and you can hear the panic in my voice. "I don't want to go alone – get Cindy too!" I whimper and cry, "I want my dad. I want to go home. I want Cindy." Vaughn asked me what they wanted, and I told him that they wanted to see inside me. "They want to learn," I said.

Then, a laparoscopy is performed and little Nancy writhes in pain. A laparoscopy is a procedure that involves a thin needle that is inserted into the abdomen allowing the doctor to see the female organs. In 1961 laparoscopies were not performed – not until the mid-

31

1980s. Vaughn questions if they are doing this procedure with malice and I quickly respond, "No, they are just doing their job."

After that procedure, they placed a smooth metal cylindrical object in my right hand, and I instinctively knew to curl my fingers around it. I felt that something was contained within this rod and that I was receiving messages or energy contained within. If you look at the illustration of me holding the rod you will see the aliens looking at the same spot above me. I believe they were looking at a monitor.

I also felt a sense of urgency, that they had limited time with me. Today in hindsight when I look at that illustration I can hear their message telling me to "Take this baton and run with it. Be an ambassador." That message and the illustration are forever linked together. For fifty years I held inside all of this information they gave me.

After a few minutes, I tell Vaughn that they are leaving the room. He asks me to describe the room. I told him that I thought the floor was white, and I was now sitting up on the table with my legs dangling over the side.

I described the doors the aliens walked through as heavy silvery metal doors that made the room seamless when they closed. I tell Vaughn that the "nice one" is babying me. I sensed the nice one was a female and said that she looked more human than the others – that her eyes are more human.

Vaughn asks if I will see her again, and I say "No, she is going to walk me out." He asks if she is going to get me home, and I tell him "no, she can't do that." Then, I told Vaughn I realized that I was right back where I started, standing right where they took me. I told him I was looking at the ship one last time, and that I was telepathically told "See? We told you we would get you back safely."

I believe now that they told me that so I would be less fearful the next time they came to get me. I tried to explain the speed at which they left. They start to go up, and then… gone. Just gone. I told Vaughn that I sit and stare out of my bedroom window every night and say, "Please come back and get me! Please come back and get me!"

Vaughn asked if I will ever see them again, and I was quickly taken back to a time in my bedroom in complete darkness, frantically trying to find my bedroom door. I felt the wall as I make my way around this now unfamiliar bedroom. Nothing was where it should be!

I tried to explain to Vaughn that they put me back "backwards." I realized then that they put me back in bed with my head at the wrong end. Thus, when I jumped up, I had gotten confused. I screamed as loud as I could, over and over, for my mom and dad.

I finally made my way to their bedroom across the hall, and dad invited me to crawl up between him and mom. They tried to tell me it was just a bad nightmare – I knew it was not, and I was mad. I lay between them, my arms crossed, almost pouting. Vaughn asked me if there was a lesson learned, and I quickly answered that "my dad can't always keep me safe all the time."

Vaughn tried to reassure me that I have protectors; loved ones that have passed, and I have guardian angels. Little Nancy argued back, "Nope! They can even get me then." Vaughn replied, "Yes, but you always survive..." Then, he asked me if I thought this had been why there had been so much anxiety in my life.

Half listening, I went on to describe all my relationships and friends as protectors. It was then that I (the adult Nancy) realized for the first time that everyone in my life had been a father figure or a mother figure, and that they had automatically taken on the role of my protector, caregiver, and at times, my financial aid source. Little girl Nancy told Vaughn in a cocky voice, "I always knew I was different from other people."

When Vaughn asked me to explain, I answered back rather smugly, "Smarter." He then asked me if that was my way of protecting myself, and I questioned him, "You mean to not let people know how smart I am?" Vaughn attempted to defend his theory by saying, "That might be a way for Nancy to protect herself." Then, adult Nancy spoke, trying to defend child Nancy, "I try to keep her safe."

Vaughn asked if it was okay for little Nancy to remember, and I responded, "I don't think I can go through with watching her suffer." Vaughn then asked me to hold little Nancy and tell her that she will be okay, and that you love her.

I held her to my chest and whimpered, "I want to take her pain away." Vaughn's comforting words carried me back to reality. He was encouraging, pointing out the progress I was making in my healing process. The session was over. Thank you, Vaughn.

The next move I made was to find Cindy, the little girl who stood by my side that day in 1961. I was determined she was going to listen to me, and she was going to talk. I had been trying to break her silence for over fifty years, always to no avail.

I now had three illustrations I knew she could not deny if I shoved them in her face! I was so determined and anxious. I feared that I would screw things up and never get her to speak. It was imperative that I handled this right. I then called her and made arrangements to go to her home praying that she would be sober. Cindy became an alcoholic, and struggled with this disease all of her life. I was very lucky that day – Cindy had not been drinking, and was sober. I was only there for a few minutes when I said "Cindy, please – I must talk to you in private."

I asked her if we could go into her bedroom and shut the door because I didn't want anything or anyone to interrupt us. She was very hesitant because she had never seen me so serious and focused.

Armed with my illustrations, I ordered her to sit on the bed across from me. I carefully removed the illustration of that day in Novi depicting the ship hovering above the tree and the car being immobilized.

Pleading, I said, "Please, Cindy. This is very important." Cindy stared at the picture. I could see fear building up inside of her. I thought to myself "Oh, no you don't! If I have to tie you to this damn bed you are going to look at these illustrations and talk to me!"

Realizing what I was doing, she recoiled a bit and screamed, "Oh, what are you doing?" I tapped the illustration with my index finger, silently commanding her to look at the illustration again. After a few seconds of silence – which felt like two hours – she finally spoke, "That's exactly how I remember it."

I then produced the second illustration showing the two of us watching the UFO and me waving my arms to get their attention. Cindy seemed to stop breathing as she looked at me, then back at the illustration and back to me.

She said, "You were gone! We couldn't find you. I think my dad called your dad because we were worried." My heart was pounding out of my chest. I couldn't believe what she had said – did she just say I was missing? I asked her, "Where did I say I had been when you found me?"

Without even one second of hesitation, she responded "Outer space!" To me, those were the most powerful words she could have spoken, and it sounded like the response of a twelve-year old child.

I then laid out the third illustration of me going up into the ship. She kept repeating, "I remember this! I remember this like it was yesterday." My eyes filled with tears, and I cried "Oh, Cindy, you have no idea how much I needed this. My life has been hell. Oh my

34

God, I thought I was crazy. I have tried so hard over the years to get you to talk about this. Thank you, Cindy."

After some time, we went to the living room where we confronted her husband Doug who was seated watching the television. I asked him to turn it off, and knelt down before him.

I produced my illustrations and we both told him about that day. It's odd that after all those years of marriage Cindy had never mentioned any of our experience to Doug. It just goes to show how much we try to hide things, even from ourselves.

Doug believed our story, he believed me. It is ironic that Doug's nickname for me was "Space Cadet." For years he never called me Nancy, just Space Cadet. After that day, he never used those words again. Instead, he referred to me as "Ensign Tremaine!" Doug became very interested in Ufology after that day, and his interest continued until his death in 2014. Thank you, Doug.

It has been nearly two weeks since I gave that envelope to Retired Chief BeGole at his street naming ceremony in Novi.

Today, the phone rings. Here is 91 year-old retired Chief BeGole calling me with a lucid memory and a sharp mind! After asking about the letter, he told me he believed the car I saw immobilized was one of his officers at the time, Martin Cone, who was off duty that evening patrolling a nearby construction site.

He told me "Honey, you're not crazy. It really happened." He also told me he believed there was an article in the Novi News about the event. He took phone calls for twenty minutes that night. One of the calls came from a city councilman's wife, and thus was to be taken seriously.   Unbelievably, everyone seems to be validating my experiences! Thank you, Chief BeGole!

On October 31, 2011, I wrote a second letter to Chief BeGole about getting something in writing covering all he could remember that day.

I let him know I realized the police records likely no longer existed, and it would make it tough for me to verify parts of my story. I told him he was the only person I had to substantiate the events of that evening. I also let him know how incredibly important his information was to me. I told him I wished I had pursued this project years ago, but was a bit afraid of what I might discover. Did he remembered any dead animals in the area?

I found a dead dog by the lake down my street. The dog was quite large and it was charred black. It had the appearance of black leather, and there were no marks or fur or paw prints in the area, nor were there any signs that there had been a fire there. I told the chief it might be radiation, but wasn't sure. I left my phone number and told him to please call me anytime with information, or if any details came to mind.

David Ames, the classmate who put me in touch with Chief BeGole, posted an anonymous letter on Facebook regarding the 1961 UFO event.

Soon after people began to take notice and respond! One woman said she remembered the incident and her parents told her not to tell anyone. Another woman posted the sighting she remembered hearing about happened in the seventies and the ship left a burn mark on the ground where it had landed, and the grass there never grew back. That report opened up another realm of possibilities. Could there have been more sightings?

An abductee must reassess everything they believed to be true. They question their place in the world. They begin to realize the government they believed in to keep them safe simply no longer exists. They realize and learn to accept just how vulnerable they are, and how they must learn how to live in a new world – a new reality – turned upside down.

For me, I have decided to welcome the aliens and learn from them. Their presence has allowed me to bring many important people into my life. I call these important people the "meant to be's". I believe we create our reality.

Harry Willnus and Vaughn Vowels are just two of the many "meant to be's" I have met. The main message I receive from the aliens who visit me is to lose the fear. We must abandon our fear of them. We are like primitives to them when confronted. We must seek to expand our relationship with them.

I have not spoken to my family about any of the high strangeness surrounding me since I began my journey in 2011. My family has never been supportive.

Even when I suffered being molested by my sister's husband my family simply turned their backs. My mother told me it was my fault. I was 14. I was told not to mention this event to my father, which added to my burden of secrets to keep. My sister decided to stay married to this man who molested me, and the family moved forward, pretending it never happened, and left me behind, pinned to that day when I was taken advantage of and molested. What he really did to me was much worse than the act itself.

36

He made me look him in the eyes and he said "Every Christmas, Thanksgiving or Holiday the family gets together, I want you to look me in the eyes and remember what "we" did." Today, I realize how he tried to make me feel like it was my fault when he used that word "we." Years later, when he tried to molest another family member, again, the family turned their backs on the accuser. He had held members of the family against their will until he finally died of cancer.

One of my biggest regrets was telling my daughter that I had undergone regression. She was aware of the UFO I saw and had also seen in Novi and in the illustrations I had drawn many times over the years.

I told her I had been abducted. She rolled her eyes at me in pure disgust and disbelief, a look I encountered so many times. I questioned her, asking, "You don't believe me?"

She responded, "I believe you believe it, everyone thinks they've been abducted!" I wanted to defend myself from such an ignorant reply but stopped dead, realizing it would be futile to try.

"Everyone thinks they've been abducted," I thought, "Did she really say that?" Being abducted is something you hold inside. I didn't say another word. I wanted to take back every single word I said. I wanted to crawl into a hole and die. I sat on her couch for several minutes in complete silence as she busied herself in the kitchen. When she finally emerged, she walked over to me, bent down and kissed me on the forehead and walked away. I felt like some pitiful animal she felt sorry for. I was so frustrated and disappointed -- I decided at that moment I would never speak about being abducted to anyone who wasn't of "like mind."

"Great spirits have always encountered violent opposition from mediocre minds."

-Albert Einstein

"Three things that cannot be long hidden: the Sun, the Moon, and the Truth."

-Buddha

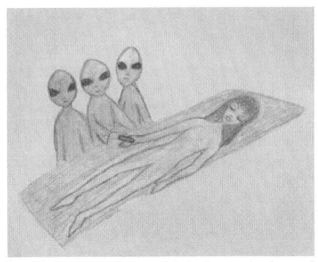

Take this baton and run with it; be an Ambassador.

Aftermath

The holidays after my sister's husband molested me were difficult to say the least. I would become depressed and physically ill before every holiday knowing how difficult it would be to lay eyes on him. I had to act like everything was normal, and that meant greeting him with a hug. It felt horrible.

Everyone in my family kisses and hugs one another. It's a tradition, and as long as I can remember, it has been that way. I would look over and see my sister glaring at me. She wanted so much to blame me for what happened.

It made me ill thinking that she stayed married to him, and it made me literally gag to think that the rest of the family thought he could do no wrong. After all, he had a great job and made lots of money, and I was just the family's black sheep, the girl who got pregnant at seventeen, the only one in the family who dropped out of school, and was divorced. Being the butt of every joke, I would often whisper under my breath, "If you only knew...."

Even in death my brother-in-law was able to reach out and hurt me. At the memorial, a tape recording he made prior to his death was played for everyone. Just hearing his voice was disgusting and disturbing. He said something about "hoping I have touched each of your lives." A deep, guttural moan came from deep within me, as if the wind had been knocked out of me. It was automatic, and it seemed to come out of nowhere.

The phone call came somewhere around 2005 or 2006. It was from my sister, and she was crying. I had not spoken to her in years, and could barely make out her words as she tried to speak and cry at the same time. I was shocked to hear her voice.

Through her tears, she said, "Oh, Nancy, I am so sorry! I always knew you were telling the truth. I have been in therapy, and my therapist told me how hard it must have been for you." I thought to myself, "You mean it took a therapist to tell her that a child being molested and having to keep the secret all her life might have psychological problems?"

Whatever the case, I was thrilled that she was acknowledging it. I figured now is better than never. We made arrangements to meet at a restaurant in Novi the following week.

We met, and both of us ordered a drink, and she began telling me how sorry she was. Then, she surprised me by asking for the details of exactly what her husband did to me. Of course, I did not share these details, and do not know why they would hold any importance to her. I told her how wonderful it will be when the family hears the truth.

Well, she stopped me dead in my tracks, saying, "I can't do that. I can't hurt my children like that. He was their father." I wondered why she even bothered to call me.

I asked her how and why she stayed married to him, and she told me it was because she was afraid of him. I realized what a selfish, thoughtless woman she was. It seemed to be only about her.

It all made sense why she was my mother's favorite – they were exactly alike. My sister *and* my mother threw me to the wolves. The only consolation I can hold onto is my belief that every life experience has been preparing me for the journey I have been on for the last four years. Everything that has occurred – the good, the bad, and the ugly were all necessary in order to prepare me and give me the knowledge, strength and experiences to draw from.

Chapter 4
Pandora's Box

On November 17, 2011, I had my third regression. Just me, Vaughn and Harry; I lovingly referred to us as the "Three Musketeers." None of us had any idea that just two days after this regression, "Pandora's Box" would be opened! The next three years will be filled with strange experiences, missing time, voids, messages, the fine-tuning of my pineal gland... and a baby.

I have never shared my regressions with anyone, and even have a very difficult time listening to them. The hardest part of writing this book was that I had to force myself to listen to them and relive them, often in the voice of "little Nancy," the child from so long ago. I was amazed at some of the things she said without hesitation, and especially her bravery.

This third regression took me back to an incident that took place in 1972 or '73, in Brighton, Michigan. I was into my second marriage, and my husband was in bed sleeping.

In retrospect, I know now that he and my daughter had been "shut down." We were renting a small duplex with a small laundry room in which there was a window above and behind the washer and dryer.

Suddenly, I heard the loudest noise, and ran to the back window. It startled me so as I stood there watching these colored lights come straight at me! It sounded like a helicopter, but the blade was in the front like an airplane.

The flashing of the colored lights was blinding, and the noise deafening – I couldn't believe how loud it was! I realized it couldn't be a helicopter or a plane, as it was flying at window level. I wondered how this thing could fly just a few feet off the ground.

I waited for it to crash into the side of the building, and then I experienced missing time, because that was the last thing I remembered until the next day. I asked my husband if he heard the noise and commotion last night, and he said he hadn't. "How could you have slept through that noise and all of the flashing lights last night," I asked. He told me he had no idea what I was talking about. I never was able to get that night out of my mind. What had happened?

Once regressed, Vaughn asked me where I was. I told him "I am standing here, I don't have any shoes on, and I am puzzled. I am just waiting. I don't see anything, but I somehow knew where I was, I just don't know how I got here."

My hands are gesturing as if to ask, "How did I get here?" I then continued, "I know where I am… I am back on the ship. Oh my God," I shouted with fear, "I don't want to go through that pain again!" and I start to cry. Vaughn assured me that I would not have to go through that pain again. He is referring to the laparoscopy.

I tell Vaughn that someone is coming and that I am scared. "I can't see them. Maybe I can't see them because I don't want to. There are two of them."

I chuckle and tell Vaughn that one of these aliens knows me, and he said "trouble" to the other one, meaning that they were going to have trouble dealing with me.

Vaughn asks me what they want with me, and I respond in a soft voice "Tests… tests." My breathing slows and I tell Vaughn they are not hurting me this time; they were just staring at me.

Vaughn asked me if I can read their minds, and I tell him, "They can read mine." I try to explain to Vaughn that they are "taking it all," meaning they were clearing my mind. I was in disbelief. I told him they were gathering information.

Vaughn asked me what kind of information they want. I tell him they are puzzled by my reactions and they are as fascinated by me as I am of them.

Vaughn asked me what it was they wanted to learn, and I told him they want to learn my thoughts and feelings.

Vaughn asked me what I told them, and I said, "I don't have to (tell them), they just take it!" At that point, Vaughn asked me if any of these events have impacted my life. I ignore the question and say, "I just don't know what happens next. I don't know…"

My breathing was labored, and I seem to be in denial of what was happening to me. I told Vaughn "They are moving… my feet aren't." I find myself between the two of them, and we are all gliding slightly above the floor together. No one's feet are moving.

I didn't know if they were holding my arms, but I did know we were all moving along in unison. I also knew they were taking me somewhere. At that point I was very upset because I realized they were going to "shut me down."

I kept on telling Vaughn this – "they were going to shut me down." I argued with them about this, and practically begged them not to, and I then realized I had no say in this at all. I was very angry with them. Vaughn asked me what it is that they don't want me to remember, and I tell him they say it will be easier this way.

Vaughn told me to be receptive and that over the course of the next few days, when I am ready to remember, the memories will return, perhaps in the form of a dream or a thought. I assured Vaughn that they were being nice to me and I realize they were doing this for my own good. Vaughn asked me where I was, and I told him "I am not anywhere. I just am."

Apparently, when they shut a person down, that person is, for lack of a better word, nowhere. They just are. They just exist.

Vaughn asked me to describe the feeling, and I replied "Paralyzed. I can't move my arms or legs – I just am."

Vaughn asked if I was a spiritual being. I replied, "I'm just me, Nancy." Vaughn then asked me if there was anything I would like to ask them, and I tell him "There is nothing. Just a wall. They have shut me down." Vaughn then suggested that the walls would come down and that the knowledge from the other side will come to me and help me to heal.

I felt my abductors apologizing for the wall, and they assure me they will help me take down these walls that have surrounded me throughout my life. I then tell Vaughn, "I am not going to be hurt anymore, and I can love now, I can love without the fear of being hurt."

I said to Vaughn, "Oh, there has been so much pain in my life." Then I am *shocked* to hear these words coming from a voice I knew to be mine, "They love me. They *are* me!"

Vaughn then told me to receive the love from them and to let it envelop me. He told me love is the most powerful force in the universe. I replied "I want to be with them forever!"

Vaughn then asked me to imagine a color and associate it with the emotion love. I say, "Blue." My breathing is slow and shallow as Vaughn speaks in his soothing voice. I trust him so.

I interrupted him to tell him that they are giving me stuff – gifts. They said I earned them. Vaughn said, "Yes, you have." Although I cannot see his face, I detect a smile in his reply.

I tell Vaughn, "I don't want to leave. I want to go with them but I can't. They tell me they are always with me, all the time." Vaughn told me they were rewarding my strengths, my courage, and even my shortcomings!

I felt myself getting angry, and realized all my feelings were coming back. I said, "They are leaving and I am right back here," to

Vaughn. I heard the disgust in my voice and the sense of resignation. Vaughn slowly brought me back to the present, and encouraged me to remember the color blue. As I came out of it, I told Vaughn I felt like I was so far away. He said I might have been in another dimension or another universe. I said in response, "It sure wasn't this one!" I was so angry to be back…

Brighton, Michigan

Chapter 5
Marriage, Memories and Messages

It is May 5, 1990, and it was the day of my fourth marriage. I had been single for a decade, so I was determined to make this marriage last. Looking back now, I recognize the many signs I chose to ignore. I truly loved him, and to this day believe it was the only time I had ever loved a man.

Our marriage, like the previous three, would last only three years. The number three seems to be the magic number for every relationship I have had. For some reason, I never seemed to make it past the first three years. My family once joked that they were going to cut the head out of a picture of my last husband, and just replace it with the head of each new man.

I was nearly six years older than him, and he would frequently remind me of that throughout our marriage. When we got married he was thrilled to have found a woman that would stay home, clean house, cook, and always look attractive. I was the "Stepford Wife."

Actually, I loved that role, and it has always been what I enjoyed doing. I took great pride in our beautiful home decorating, and its immaculately clean condition. My days were spent cleaning, going to the gym, shopping, and cooking him a four-course meal every single day.

We had a time share and would spend one weekend a month out of state where he could play golf, and I could go shopping. Other weekends would be spent going out dancing or going out for dinner. I really couldn't have asked for more. Everything went well until one day he came home from work and I was still in my workout clothes, and he noticed the new muscles I was developing.

"It must be nice to work out every day and not do a fucking thing," he said. I reminded him that I was working when we met, and that he insisted I quit my job when we got married.

He said the money I was making was a joke and we would not be able to travel if I continued to work. We were living the life we both signed up for. I let the remark slide, but he also noticed that my new muscles had given me a new confidence.

He started to feel it necessary to make nasty little remarks in hopes to keep me in my place. One summer afternoon we spent the day in our back yard just enjoying the sun. I was looking at him and I was thinking of how much I loved this man. He then looked at me and said "You are nothing but a forty-year-old woman who has never done a fucking thing with her life."

Those words were beyond any pain I can describe. I held back tears behind my sunglasses. When he got up to trim the hedges I walked through the back door and straight to the bedroom where I scooped up some clothes and my purse. I left out the front door and went to my daughter's place where I would stay.

He called me there several times and told me to "get my ass home where I belonged" and that I was *his* wife. As far as I was concerned, he killed any feelings I had for him.

I eventually went back to my home because I felt like I was invading my daughter's space, and I had no money to help out. When I returned home, things were not the same as they were.

After a short while I told him I was going to have my hair lightened. He forbade me to do it. I had black hair all my life and wanted a change. I went to have my hair done in a medium auburn color. It looked great, and I loved it. I knew when he saw it he would feel the same way.

I started preparing dinner as he walked through the door from work. I smiled at him waiting for him to say "Wow! That looks great!" Instead, he just gave me a dirty look and went into the bedroom to change clothes for dinner. While he was changing, the phone rang – it was my girlfriend in Canada. I excitedly told her about my hair.

She asked me what my husband thought of it, and I told her "he hasn't said." Without warning, I felt an arm backslap me across the face knocking the phone out of my hand.

The phone swung by its cord falling to the floor. I landed on my ass. He said, "I'm gonna kill you. I'm gonna beat you to a fuckin' bloody pulp." I crawled as fast as I could until I built up enough momentum to stand up and run to the bedroom where the other phone was.

All I could think of was grabbing the phone in the bedroom and yelling to my girlfriend to, "Call the police!" I barely got those words out when he took the phone out of my hands and slammed me in the head with it.

The last thing I remember before passing out was him standing on the bed holding me by the neck of my shirt and the waist on my pants and swinging me back and forth until he was rocking me like a pendulum. When he had me at a good speed, he threw me into the air off the back of the bed. I didn't have time to put my arms out in front of me to break my fall, and so I landed face down on our beautiful white carpet.

I don't know how long I was out, but when I raised my head I saw blood on the carpet, and my husband standing guard at the bedroom door with his hands blocking my exit. I looked at him and I started to cry. Our marriage had just ended. There was nothing he could ever say or do to make this go away. Then, there was a loud banging on the door, "Police, police open up!"

I now live in a small one-bedroom apartment and spend much of my time alone. My apartment is immaculate and everything is in its place. Organization is the only thing I have any control of.

I quit eating red meat and smoking around 1994 and my exercise routine consists of Pilates and swimming three times a week. I believe being limber is the key to youth. The day you can no longer bend down to pick something up off the floor without trouble is a sign your body is breaking down.

I am in perfect physical health except for high blood pressure when exposed to a doctor or a nurse. In their presence, my blood pressure has been as high as 195! At home, my blood pressure is normal, but the doctor does not believe me when I tell him because twice a year when I must see him to get my prescription for anxiety medication refilled, my blood pressure is sky-high! It's a forty-five minute drive to his office, and by the time I get there I am sweating and in a panic.

I haven't had a pap smear in over twenty years, and I will never have another one. I do everything I can to avoid going to doctors, even passing a kidney stone on two separate occasions on my own. I have what is called "White Coat Syndrome."

When I was seventeen, the gynecologist that delivered my daughter molested me. It happened during my six-week checkup after my daughter's birth. He sent the nurse out of the room – she knew what was to happen. My mother-in-law was waiting outside in the car for me.

When I came out of the office and she saw me, she knew something was wrong – I was shaking uncontrollably. When we got home, she called the doctor's office and there was a lot of screaming. I loved her for that. However, it was never spoken of again. It is there in my medical records. I hate the word molested – it sounds so innocent and harmless. It was rape!

I wish I could put his name in this book for everyone to see. He is retired now, but he is still alive. I know there are many victims of his out there. Molestation is never a one-time thing. A molester seeks out his victims. Over the years I have met several women that have also been molested by their doctors or family members...I know people would be shocked to know the truth of it all.

I married four abusive men. I have dated abusive men – too many to mention. I have never had a romantic relationship that lasted more than three years. Since my last divorce in 1993, I ended that cycle and I haven't been in any abusive relationships. Unfortunately, all anyone hears is that I was married four times. When I was single for forty years, people will still only recall that I was married four times. People who commit murder are exonerated after less time! I am proud to say I am no longer a victim.

I have never needed the company of others. I do enjoy the company of others, but I can only tolerate so much physical or emotional contact. If I become overwhelmed or if I am away from my apartment (my "home plate") for too long, I hurry home to close and lock my doors and draw the curtains. It can take two or three days to "recharge my batteries." Even as a child I would lock myself in the bathroom of our house to escape my siblings. I am quite the quirky character. Since putting down my cat named "Cuddle Bugs," my companion for nearly nineteen years, I live with a stuffed black cat and a mannequin.

Dr. Willnus realized the strong need I had to be with people who were of "like-kind," so he suggested I go to a few MUFON (Mutual UFO Network) meetings. It was at one of these meetings I would meet a lady named Landi Mellas, an experiencer who grew up not too far from where I lived. She is also the author of a book called *The Other Sky*, about her experiences. I purchased a copy of her book and she wrote inside the cover "Do not hide from who you are." We had a wonderful connection, and I was thrilled to have met her. We also attended a few abductee group meetings. Thank you, Landi, for helping me heal.

On November 9, 2011, two days after my third regression, I was telepathically told that I would now not only be able to remember the entire event back in 1961, but to relive it. Just as they had promised me they would return the memories to their rightful owner, the experiencer, the one who lived that experience – me! Below are some of the messages I received, both telepathically, and through the computer.

As I was taken through the events of that day I would be stopped periodically and directed toward the computer. I was told to "Stop... read... learn..."

Other times, I would be given messages via telepathy. I do not recall any words or letters I typed to arrive at any of this information. It was not until after the progression, and to this day, when I read the messages, I appreciate them so much. This lasted for over seven hours, and I don't remember once getting up off the floor where I was seated in front of the computer.

My pad of paper and pen rested on the floor within arm's reach because I was frequently instructed to put pen to paper! This is a process they utilize with me to this day! This is often how I receive messages. Sometimes my ears will start to ring, and occasionally, there will be no warning at all, just the words "put pen to paper."

I write their message down and have no idea what they mean until much later, and a few are self-explanatory. I believe these messages are from a collective mind, or from an entity I call Mr. This entity was the pilot of the ship that visited me in 1961. Mr. and I have a symbiotic relationship and I will talk about this relationship a little further along.

Inside the Ship

On that evening back in 1961, I entered the ship and ran right past the pilot. I was not afraid. The pilot, who looks like anyone's father, did not frighten me. He was seated, and I know he was in charge, and he flies "this thing." I thought to myself, "I can't believe I am in a flying saucer!"

The pilot was amused, and corrects me, "It is a ship." My hands went to my hips in defiance and I replied, "Mr., this can't be a ship because a ship goes in the water, and a ship was what Captain Hook was on." "Oh," he replied, "but this does go into the water!"

This short exchange of words would help me put a date to this event, and it also gave the pilot a name. I still call him "Mr." The play "Peter Pan" with Mary Martin had just premiered on television for the first time in December of 1960 and I watched it with my family. Captain Hook and the crocodile scared me so much that my parents threatened to turn the production off. Even though it scared me back then, it was and still is my favorite play. I still have two of the songs from the play on my IPod. I find it ironic that Dr. Harry Willnus has one arm – just like Captain Hook! Coincidence?

Now standing inside the ship I clearly saw that the red, green, and white lights I perceived on the outside of the ship were actually windows – very large windows that ran the entire circumference of the ship. I stand on my toes to look out the window, and I can see Mr. Lutes, Cindy's father standing there looking up. To no avail I waved and hollered to him – I see no one else. The police and Cindy are also gone.

Fortunately, as part of this regression I am spared having to relive the laparoscopy. I think they felt reliving through in one regression was enough.

I am then taken forward to the "nice one." She was the one female on board who babied me, helped me get dressed, and walked me back to the pilot. As I approached him I felt confused and angry. "Mr., why did you let them hurt me?" I asked.

Mr. told me that my pain was only perceived, and this infuriated me. He then went on to explain to me that perception is the way each of us define our reality, and that there was more than one way to perceive things.

He told me to learn to expand my perception and find the positives in each perception. Then, I am directed to the computer and I read these words: "If we are abused, then we perceive our reality as negative. Through love we are able to perceive our reality as positive and find that it is so. Everything and everybody is peripheral to our universe and our reality. If we can conquer the concept that we are all part of one energy, the concept of unity becomes obvious to us and we no longer fear the unknown or death because whatever we are, we are always who we are."

Then, I was directed to read two quotes from Albert Einstein: "Great spirits have always encountered violent opposition from mediocre minds," and a second quote, "In light of knowledge attained, the happy achievement seems almost a matter of course and any intelligent student can grasp it without too much trouble."

But the years of anxious searching in the dark with their intense longing, their alternations of confidence and exhaustion and their final emergences into the light – only those who have experienced it can understand it."

I believe the first quote was shown to me to prepare me for the obstacles I would have to overcome in the telling of my story. The second quote confirms the progress I have made.

Next, I read the following: "People can recover from learned helplessness. Turn on all your positive sensors and believe in your ability to change and grow." As I turned from the computer, these words were put into my head, and I was told to commit them to paper: "All memories are packed and taken with us into each new life. When the load becomes too heavy, we travel as (or become) 'light knowledge energy.'"

I found this fascinating, and I still do. Again, this message was given to me in 2011 and again during the 2012 UFO Congress. One of the speakers mentioned that the aliens were able to travel as "light energy." I leaned over to Dr. Willnus and said "He forgot the word *knowledge*." "Yes," said Harry, "And that word is important to their message. In the future, when you begin to doubt yourself remember this."

The last time I was directed to the computer during this regression Mr. felt it important and necessary for me to know that a meeting between the aliens and Eisenhower did indeed take place. I found myself trembling as I read these words: "'The Eisenhower Treaty' was agreed to by both parties on the 20th of February, 1954."

It is my understanding that there was more than one meeting involving aliens. However, I have a problem believing some of the following sentences listed below. Believe what you will but there was a meeting with Eisenhower and the aliens. Mr. wanted to make that very clear to me.

1. The aliens would not interfere in our affairs, and we would not interfere in theirs.

2. We would keep their presence on Earth a secret, and in return they would furnish us with advanced technology, and we would receive assistance from them in our technological advancement.

3. They would not make any other treaty with the Earth Nation.

4. They could abduct humans on a limited basis for the purpose of medical examinations and to monitor our development with the stipulation that humans would not be harmed and they would be returned to their point of abduction.

5. Humans would retain no memory and that the Alien Nation would furnish the MJ-12 Committee with a list of human contacts and abductees on a regular basis.

They kept their promise of my having no memories for fifty years, and they chose to return those memories to me. Whoever is sending the messages seems to be very concerned with my well-being. I feel loved, and I feel me loving me. After that third regression, I began receiving messages. It is my belief that these messages come from a "collective mind" or from Mr. Here is a list of some of the messages I received in the beginning of my journey:

1. "If you want to know who we are, you have only to look in the mirror. We are you – we are all one."

2. "Your destiny is to learn what you are, and then express it perfectly."

3. "Empathy holds back technology. It is important to realize the driver still lives. It is the vehicle that is sacrificed."

4. "Thoughts are real and have a creative energy."

5. "Imagine the human body as the Universe. The Universe has cancer."

6. "The pyramids are a house to harness energy."

7. "Whatever we are, we are always who we are."

8. "The body is a sending and receiving antenna."

9. "Our messages are not for everyone. Many will be left behind." (*I didn't think this message was to be taken literally, but in 2014 I was told that is was.*)

10. "Oh how truly fast we grow when we truly want to know."

11. "You need more love than a human can provide; that is why with a man you are never satisfied."

12. "We can guide you, but we can never lead you."

13. "You are clearing a path for others. The obstacles are placed to slow you down so you can learn."

14. "Do not look back – but leave pebbles to help others find their way."

15. "Pray with your heart, listen with your heart."

16. "Your mission is not to convince, but to inform."

17. "Through love we are able to perceive our reality as positive."

18. "When family and friends no longer see your renewed strength as smug superiority they will come to terms with their own truths."

19. "Love in its purest form is given, not received."

20. "We are here to avert war. We are here to save you from yourselves."

21. "You must learn to rule by love, not fear."

22. All memories are packed and taken with us in each new life. When the load becomes too heavy, we travel (or become) "light knowledge energy."

There have been so many times I would doubt my sanity and myself. How could all this be real? Was it really happening? It was then I would reach out to Vaughn for validation. Here is one of his beautiful responses:

Nancy,

I am so sorry I did not get back to you sooner. Yes, I read your email. If you are crazy, then so are a hundred thousand other experiencers. There is nothing I have heard you say or do to make me doubt your sanity. Our government is guilty of not supporting its citizens who have gone through these harrowing episodes. The messages coming through you are of great value to humanity. Those who are capable of understanding spiritual evolution will benefit. I am impressed with your courage and drive for the truth. Mediocre minds are only impressed with the mediocre.

Sincerely,

Vaughn Vowels

Thank you, Vaughn

Chapter 6
Meet Skinny Bob, Sid, Mr., and Drax

In the beginning of 2012 and shortly after my third regression, I was allowed to remember the conversation I had with my father in 1961 after the Novi, Michigan experience, on that particular summer night. My father was kneeling down on the kitchen floor, and we had our arms wrapped around each other. We held each other very tightly.

He reassured me that I was home, and I was safe but I somehow knew he wasn't totally convinced of that. I was very aware of his deep concern and he was very aware that I had been traumatized. He told me that I should not speak of what I had seen or what had happened – ever. I was confused, "But why? I want to!" "You can't, do you understand me?"

He then grabbed me firmly by the forearms shaking me to further reinforce his demand, "Do you understand me, do you?" I started to cry and said "Yes," assuring him I would remain silent. I did not understand why my father was saying these things and why he seemed angry with me. I didn't understand why this event was to be kept secret, and from whom?

I now realize that my father's anger was coming from a place of fear. I believe now that someone had already talked to my dad and warned him to silence me. It worked, because I held this secret for fifty years.

I must have talked to my father about the aliens I saw on the ship, because at some point that evening my dad felt it necessary to tell me about "Skinny Bob," an alien he said the government had captured and was given that nickname.

I clearly remember he said "captured." I had always assumed it was our government who captured Skinny Bob, but the Russians, known as the Soviets at that time, were claiming responsibility for Skinny Bob's capture. None of it mattered to me.

The words "captured" and "Skinny Bob" angered me. Even as a child I realized how cruel and mean that was, and I expressed what I felt to my father. People question the credibility of the "Skinny Bob" videos one can see today on YouTube, but you cannot take away the fact that my father told me about Skinny Bob fifty years before those videos surfaced.

The original Skinny Bob videos were first seen in 2011. All of this information was not to be shared with anyone – not even my mother. It was our secret. How did my father know about Skinny Bob? I believe he learned of Skinny Bob during World War II. Again, I wondered why my father told me about Skinny Bob, and I figured he told me because it validated my experiences. It would be of great value and reassuring information for me, and it has been. Thank you so much, dad.

My father served in the 5th Air Corp during World War II, and spent three years away in New Guinea, the Philippines and the Netherland East Indies.

He was in over one hundred air raids, and some of those air raids were shared with "Pappy Gunn," an expert in low-level, daredevil flying who was recognized for numerous acts of heroism. My dad drove a truck for the Air Corp delivering and hauling essential supplies. He also drove General Whitehead and General Prentice to Tokyo to see how bad the city was ruined, and to pick out places for the occupation troops to live in.

It was the era of the "Foo Fighter," a term used by Allied aircraft pilots that witnessed these mysterious balls of light. I sent for my father's military records in hopes I might find something. I was not really sure what it was I might find. I received a letter from the National Personnel Records Center dated January 29, 2015, telling me that my father's records had been destroyed in a fire. Well, I have much of my father's military paperwork, as well as the three years' worth of love letters he wrote to my mom while he was in the service.

When my mom came home that night, my silence was further enforced. I remember that night and many nights after standing on the headboard in my bedroom chanting over and over again, "Please come back and get me, please come back and get me." I wonder now why I would have said that. I think I knew I belonged to them. It must have been a very positive feeling they left me with. I found it strange that they would take my memories of being aboard the ship away but leave my longing and desire to be with them.

Sid

Sid is not his name. It is an acronym for *Someone I Dated*. Sid found me on a dating site. The date was January 7, 2012. I gave him my phone number and we wound up chatting for hours. We decided to meet at a nearby restaurant a few days later. I could not believe how tall he was! He looked like a giant. Although he claimed to be six feet five inches tall, in his profile he was another inch taller!

54

He claimed he did that because he did not want to brag. I figure he did it because he is so much taller than average – taller than I and most women prefer to date. I barely make five feet and three inches tall. I like tall men, but his height made me not only uncomfortable, but also embarrassed.

Everywhere we went, people would gasp at the contrast between the two of us. I was barely one hundred five pounds, and he was at least two hundred fifty! He would yawn almost continuously during our first date even though I felt he was crazy about me. I found out later he yawns all the time – perhaps due to the lack of oxygen way up there! Sid was far from the type of man I would normally be attracted to. He was an uncomplicated and uneducated man with terrible grammar, and I found myself constantly correcting him. He didn't mind, in fact he encouraged it.

Sid's father died when he was only a few weeks old and his mother never remarried, so he grew up without a father figure. They were very poor, and Sid had a hard time being teased in school about his clothes and his height. After high school he joined the Army, and after the Army, he took a position working as a prison guard. To this day he still lives in the same area he grew up in, and he kept the same job for twenty years.

Because of his size, I was naturally afraid that if he ever got angry he could easily hurt me or even kill me. I asked him as I ask every man if he had ever been physically abusive, and like every man I ever met he said no. He was quick to say "not physically…" but that he was currently in therapy for anger management issues. I would later find out it was because he had threatened and intimidated his ex-wife's boyfriend at a sporting event for one of his sons.

If you look in the dictionary for passive-aggressive, you will see Sid's picture. His anger, I later learned, was focused mainly at himself. He had no self-esteem, and he would pout and throw temper tantrums just like a child if he didn't get his way. It was hilarious to see this giant of a man with his lower lip stuck out, giving me the silent treatment!

He never raised a hand to me, and I knew he never would. He sure knew how to make life miserable though. There were three things Sid lived for: sex, sports, and food! Outside of that there existed no further depth to his personality.

There was one thing I couldn't figure out. There was an intense sexual energy between us that I could not explain. His height and size might have bothered me out of bed, but in bed he was very exciting. I felt feminine and overpowered. I wanted to do everything and anything with him, and I really do not know how I held off until the third date. My imagination ran wild, and our sexual encounters were anything but conventional. We could not keep our hands off of each other.

Sid had absolutely no knowledge of UFOs, abductions or aliens. He had never heard of Betty and Barney Hill, and never even heard of the movie Close Encounters of the Third Kind. I attempted to educate him the best I could, but it was a period of time when I was still learning as well.

Whenever I brought up the subject of UFOs, he would practically fall asleep. I would watch him struggling to listen to me, but even my best efforts were futile. I finally came to believe that "they" might actually be causing him to tune me out. Sid had absolutely no interest in hearing about any of it. At times, his disinterest caused me to become so very frustrated with him!

Five days after meeting Sid I had my fourth regression. This was the session I deleted by accident (I still question this). To make matters worse, I had no memory – I couldn't remember anything about that regression.

I sent an email to Vaughn asking him if he could recall anything about it for this book. He didn't get back to me before I was to be interviewed live on the air by the Starborn Support Radio hosts.

I asked Michael Melton, the host, if he would allow Vaughn Vowels to join me on his show for support, and he recommended that he do so. Their producer, Jamie Havican, agreed to bring him on the show as a guest. When I listened to Vaughn talking to the host about that fourth regression, I became aware of what was discussed. Sex bites? Was Sid a "Sex Bite?" Everything that follows will certainly confirm that.

I have dreaded writing this book because of the reaction I might get to the material in it. Over the past three years I have tried to discuss this with a few people and *no one* understood or got the meaning. I couldn't understand why. I was even told to leave this information out of the book. I considered it, but this information is extremely vital in understanding the Reptilian agenda.

Other women think I'm bragging or exaggerating, and men cannot get past the sexual content and their wild imaginations enough to understand. I never even get to finish the story before they change the subject or I become so uncomfortable that I have to stop the conversation. I do not want this phenomenon to define me or become the main focus of this book.

I did research on what I was experiencing and I promise you that I have not found a single woman my age or any age for that matter whose experiences even come close to what happened to me. If there is someone out there who experienced similar phenomena to mine, I pray she will come forward. I am so very grateful that these experiences have ended.

There is a fine line between pleasure and pain. As I understand it now, the Reptilians are attempting to incorporate sexual desire back into themselves or into their hybrids, Reptilian-Humans. The facts are not entirely clear yet.

They somehow managed to manipulate my pineal gland and by doing so, they were able to experience my pleasure, and I believe Sid's pleasure as well. It really got out of control on February 8, 2012. It was difficult putting the right words together to describe the following. I've done the best I can and I hope you, the reader, will be able to understand the facts I am trying to convey through my direct experiences, trying to tell the absolute truth about what happened, because this is just one part of a much bigger picture.

On that day in February while having sex with Sid I experienced at least thirty ejaculations in rapid succession. I could not control or stop them. The best way to explain what was happening to me is to liken it to an automatic weapon being fired. I also experienced at least five to ten orgasms. Understand that these sensations are separate from each other. The entire situation was unhealthy and out of control. I had lost well over a quart of body fluids. At one point I clutched my heart and exclaimed, "Ouch! That really hurt!" There was only one very sharp pain.

All physical contact between Sid and I ceased right then and there. My heart was pounding and racing as if it were going to burst from my rib cage. After an hour or so I sent Sid home so I could go to the tanning salon in preparation for the 2012 UFO Congress I was going to attend. As I was driving to the salon, my heart had not slowed down and it was beating at an unhealthy speed. I could practically hear it beating.

I was becoming more and more concerned and then decided to call my girlfriend Cindy. She was quick to tell me I was likely having a heart attack, and that I should go directly to the hospital. I was not in any pain – how could it be a heart attack? I didn't care for her assessment, so I called my best friend Tom.

I was always able to tell Tom everything, but perhaps this was a bit much, and so much deeper than anything we had ever discussed before. Despite the depth, he said that he agreed with Cindy -- I was probably having a heart attack, and he quickly reminded me of my father's heart trouble and that he had suffered numerous heart attacks. Yes, I thought, but my father smoked and drank, was overweight and did not eat well. There are no words I can use to describe the fear I felt as I walked into the emergency room. I had only one thought… *Needles!* I have never been able to watch another person get an injection – even on the television!

As I parked my car in the hospital lot, the thought entered my head that I might be here a while. When I entered the emergency room there was a woman seated at the admittance desk. I walked up to the counter, bent over and said, "It's probably nothing, but I might have had a heart attack."

Well, you never saw people suddenly scramble into action so quickly! The next thing I knew, I was in a wheelchair and was whisked away to a back room where two female nurses snatched my driver's license.

The very first question one of the nurses asked was, "What happened?" I said, "I cannot tell you – it is too embarrassing." The nurse insisted, "Well, you must tell us." I finally broke down and told them about the many ejaculations and orgasms I experienced. I also told them I had lost at least a quart of body fluids.

The nurses looked at each other, and started laughing out loud. Laughing out loud! "Sure you did, honey," one of them quipped. "Well, good for you," the other nurse followed up. Now, I was irate, "I am telling you the truth!" They both left the room and returned with a man I assumed was a physician. I later found out he was a physician's assistant. He proceeded to sit down beside a monitor located by my bed.

"Tell him. Tell him what you told us," the one nurse said. I felt as if I was being mocked.

"No," I insisted. The nurses told me I had to, and they both had big grins on their faces.

"Please," I pleaded with them, "…can't you tell him for me? I am too embarrassed." They insisted I tell the P.A. I made eye contact with him and they apparently told him because he was looking at me as if I was crazy.

"What happened," he said, with a truly condescending tone. I stumbled over my words as I told him about the many ejaculations and orgasms I experienced, and my heart would not stop racing.

I repeated, "My heart won't stop racing!" The nurses kept telling the physician's assistant how high my blood pressure was. I told them I suffer from post-traumatic stress disorder and "white coat syndrome."

"I am having a panic attack," I added. I cannot tell you how many times they asked me what my pain level was, and I kept telling them "Zero."

I explained further that there had been one very sharp pain after my last orgasm and ejaculation, and that was the extent of it.

They absolutely refused to believe that I wasn't in any pain and even made a point of stating in my medical records that I had been in pain for an hour and a half.

One of the nurses placed a nitroglycerin pill under my tongue, and the P.A. attached the monitor by my bed on me, and about a minute later he said, "You had a heart attack."

I grabbed his arm and insisted he repeat what he just said. He repeated in the exact same words, "You had a heart attack." He told me he was sending me to a larger facility at a second hospital for care, as they were not prepared to handle cardiac emergencies.

I couldn't believe it; I was in shock. I felt as if life had ended for me right then. I asked the nurse for my purse so I could use my cell phone to make calls to family and friends, and I asked for privacy. I called my daughter and my best friend Tom.

I simply told them I had a heart attack. I did not call Sid and I did not want him notified. I felt I had been given a death sentence. Soon, a stretcher was brought into the room and I was wheeled out to a crowd of about a dozen doctors and nurses, and God only knows whom else, and there were big grins on all of their faces.

"You told them," I said to one of the nurses, "I can't believe it – you told everyone!" It seems that everyone wanted to see the crazy sixty-two year old woman that claimed to do the impossible! I never saw so much nudging and grinning. I seemed to have been a joke.

Once I was at the second hospital which was affiliated with the first I was administered more drugs. It was obvious by the way I was being treated that word had already gotten out about my "sexual abilities" and me.

Tom would later laugh and say "You were famous in that hospital!" I didn't find it funny, and I was appalled at the fact there was no confidentiality between doctor or nurse, and patient. Every nurse that entered my room wanted me to describe what had happened. I thought, "What the fuck?" I was mortified!

The following day I was wheeled into the operating room for a procedure called a heart catheterization. This procedure is very invasive, and I had already made it clear that no matter what they found there would be *no cutting*!

I also made it clear that I wanted the catheter put into my arm and not my thigh. I was crying hysterically. I was terrified. The next thing I remember is waking up in recovery, and the doctor saying, "There is absolutely nothing wrong with you!" I asked, "You mean I didn't have a heart attack?"

He replied, "Not unless some kind of miracle was performed." Inside my head I thought, "Was some kind of a miracle performed?"

When they wheeled me out of the operating room my daughter and Tom were standing there and Tom was holding a diagram of my heart signed by the doctor who performed the procedure. "Dr. Steele," it was signed, and next to his signature he had written in big letters "NORMAL." I kept this as a souvenir.

"My daughter said reassuringly, "There is nothing wrong with you, mom!" I should have been pleased – even elated, but I was furious, and on the warpath!" I went through that pain and the needle – that damn needle for nothing?

I wanted out of there, and I wanted to go home immediately. A young female doctor came into my room and said they wanted to keep me overnight because my blood pressure was so low. "Really," I said, "Low?" I added, "That's because you've been popping pills down my throat since yesterday!"

I demanded they allow me to sign out that very minute. The doctor actually apologized, saying that the P.A. really thought I suffered a heart attack because of something he saw on the monitor.

I angrily said to her "Had you all listened to me and believed me, I would have never had to go through all of this!" The doctor apologized again, and told me I probably just had a "heart spasm."

I replied rather smugly, "Ya think? I think at least 30 ejaculations and several orgasms would have killed a fucking twenty year old!"

She smiled and nodded. Soon after, I was on my way home. My hospital release paper says it was, "probably a heart spasm." At any rate, it was a relief to know that my heart was in perfectly good condition. It was a good thing as well, because for over a year after this episode, every time Sid and I had sex, I would experience multiple orgasms and ejaculations and enormous losses of fluids.

February 22-27, my friend Nicole and I were in Arizona for the 2012 UFO Congress. I was fascinated with one particular mountain in Arizona and told her I knew there were Reptilians working inside that mountain.

I said to her "This is my home," referring to Arizona and this mountain. I never wanted to leave, and have dreamed of living there ever since. Sometime after I got home from Arizona, Sid and I were making love, and out of nowhere, I just blurted out "I'm pregnant, and it's a boy!" Sure enough, in the weeks that followed, my stomach grew. I never doubted for a minute that I was pregnant – never told a soul except for Sid, and he never did understand. He humored me and to this day I resent him for that.

On March 8, 2012, I had the dry heaves for nearly 24 hours straight. I lay on the bathroom floor with nothing but my pillow. I knew it was morning sickness because I suffered with it for the first few months I was pregnant with my daughter.

On March 9, 2012, Sid booked a local hotel room, and purchased tickets to see the comedian "Larry the Cable Guy." "Larry" was not quite my idea of humor – Sid and I really had nothing in common except sex. Now I was still weak from the previous night, but Sid insisted I go to the show. I went without protest because I did not want to be subjected to his pouting lips and silent treatment. He never believed I had morning sickness!

After the show we went back to our room, and I got into bed. Sid stood at the opposite side of the bed, and I watched his eyes roll up. He then collapsed onto the bed with his head in the center of the mattress and his feet hanging off the bed. He had all of his clothes on, and his mouth was hanging open.

I yelled at him and tried to move him, but he was dead weight. I placed my feet in the center of his stomach and pushed with all my might, but he wouldn't budge.

Then a calm feeling came over me and I lied back on the pillow and said, "Wake up, Sid. They are coming to get me. They are coming to get me…" I recall not feeling afraid, and I wanted Sid to see them. But, even if he had seen them, he would not have believed it.

I watched the window in the room, waiting for them to come so I could welcome them. That was around midnight. At 5:00 the next morning, I awoke and felt a presence inside the room. I knew if I peeked, I would see who it was. So, I squinted slightly and there he was -- a small grey alien! He was making circular motions over my stomach with his right hand. I still find it odd that realizing he was right handed was something that stood out to me. He told me telepathically "I am making one last check on the baby..." I felt a true sense of love and concern coming from this being.

Finally, Sid came to and he had a bewildered look on his face. He looked around the room assessing where he was and what had apparently happened.

"They took me," I told him. He did not understand what I was saying. "They took me and they shut you down." I could tell he was totally oblivious to what I was saying. "Don't you find it odd that it is five o'clock in the morning, it's our first night in the hotel, and you still have your clothes on?"

On March 25, 2012, I was given the name of my son. He would be called "Drax." The name was placed in my head. I sent Sid a text telling him the name of our son and wondered why I even bothered telling him anything, and why in God's name they chose him to be a part of this process.

Mr.

I had drawn an illustration of Mr. somewhere between the third and fourth regression. I honestly had no idea what I was drawing until the picture was done. Days later I was told to write below the picture "See me as I am."

"… see me as I am."

I knew nothing about the Reptilian race, and I had never heard of "shape shifting." That subject matter was far beyond the scope of my research. It wasn't until I showed my illustration to someone at a MUFON meeting and saw her reaction to it. I realized people's perception of Reptilians was not exactly positive in nature.

She asked, "Is he a Reptilian?" "Yes," I replied, "I guess – why?" That is when I started to hear how awful and demonic Reptilians were. I would later show this illustration to a few people at the Abductees Group Meeting, and they told me he was a "Draconian Reptilian." I got the same negative responses.

Whatever he was, I loved him. I found myself defending Mr., and to this day, I continue to defend him. I am grateful for the opportunity to work with the Reptilians and to been given information to share with others. I see them as parents and teachers. I might not be happy with all they do to me, but I compare it to when my parents would take me for inoculations or to have my tonsils out. Things that are good for you don't always feel good.

I need to make it clear that Mr. does not reveal himself as the Draconian Reptilian he is. It is only by the illustration I drew that I know how he looks and the words he had me write beneath his illustration "See me as I am" that I acknowledge his physical appearance. I do, however, recall one event when I was very young sitting next to him and staring at his face, which was filled with scales – the scales bothered me so much that I wanted to scratch them off. Mr. stands about seven to eight feet tall, and is a brownish green color with scales. He has a very thick tail that rests on the floor. He has webbed feet and three long clawed fingers and a thumb. His eyes are amber, and he can look right through you. He exudes love, power and leadership. He is a very proud creature, and is well respected by all species of aliens. I know that I belong to him. The only way to describe our relationship is "symbiotic." We have always been together it seems, and always will be. I am reminded of that silly line of prose he put inside my head: "You need more love than a human can provide. That is why with a man you are never satisfied..."

The only aliens that have ever shown themselves to me are the greys, the female hybrid, my son Drax, and my daughter. All communication with Mr. is done telepathically – I do not see him physically, but I do feel his presence and his love. Mr. and I are able to communicate by thought and feelings, so there is no need for physical form.

What makes us any different from them? We are now living in a world where robots are taking over many of our jobs. Robots will build houses, drive cars, and take care of the elderly. Through Cryogenics, we might soon be able to bring the dead back to life. We will soon be able to load our consciousness into a computer – a complete thought transfer, which will allow us to live and communicate forever. We have been inbreeding animals for decades. What makes us any different than the Reptilians? Some of us play God every day. Nothing is different except for the fact that they are far more advanced than we are, and they are using their abilities for the *good* of mankind, and for the *good* of this planet we call home. I am again reminded of one of their messages:

> *"If you want to know who we are, you have only to look in the mirror. We are you..."*

I do know that they, the Reptilians and Mr., are able to experience the emotions of anxiety, fear and sexual pleasure through me and know that their main function is the study of genetics. I believe they are doing some much needed upgrading at this time, and they are in the process of removing the emotions associated with hate, rage, and the desire for war and murder. These are emotions of no value to society. We must learn to rule by love, not fear. I am hesitant to say they created us because I am met with such resistance.

It's Easter Day, April 8, 2012. I managed to hide my pregnancy from my family. If they had noticed, at least no one said anything to me. I stopped at my best friend Tom's house to wait for him to come home. I was going to spend the night instead of making the hour-long drive home in the dark, and I was tired.

I put on my pajamas and noticed just how large my stomach was. I quickly grabbed my phone and took pictures. I sent one to Sid who was shocked at how much bigger my stomach was compared to a few days ago. Tom arrived home, and I greeted him at the door.

He immediately looked down and said, "What's up with your stomach?" I lifted my pajama top just enough to show him my swollen stomach, and told him "I am pregnant..." Silence ensued as Tom tried to process what I had just said. Finally, Tom said with concern and astonishment "Well, you... you better stop being pregnant!" That was the end of the discussion.

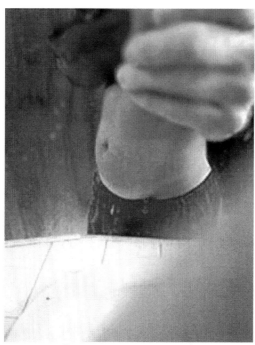

Pregnant with Drax

Four days later, I had a scheduled regression with Vaughn – the twelfth of April. Vaughn and Harry were sent emails asking if I could reschedule. I never understood why I didn't tell them about the pregnancy, and why I worked so hard to keep it from both of them. I believe I was somehow programmed not to tell them. It is only in hindsight that I realize this. It is now apparent that they did not want any interference with my pregnancy.

End of the Pregnancy

On April 15th, they took Drax. I could be a day or two off, because things were fuzzy and my memory, perception and senses were affected at the time. I felt empty. My stomach was flat again and I felt empty both physically and emotionally.

I knew Drax was never really mine and knew they would take him. I asked them why they had taken my baby, and they told me they had "claimed" him.

I found the word "claimed" an odd word to use, so I did a little investigation; I Googled it. I knew what "claimed," meant, but like every other word, there are other more uncommon definitions listed below the most obvious one. The best alternative definition I could find was "to assert one's ownership."

I asked them how they managed to get me pregnant in the first place. I was given a mental image of a large bowl with a large spoon making stirring motions. I understood that to mean Drax was a combination of me, Sid and Mr. I did ask them that I be allowed to see my son and be a part of his life. They granted that wish.

On May 18, 2012, I would have my final regression with Vaughn. This regression would cause a split of the "Three Musketeers," and our relationships would never be the same.

For well over a year, Vaughn and I would go our separate ways. Not until I listened to this regression for the purpose of this book would I be able to understand. Even my relationship with Harry would change.

Once regressed, Vaughn begins the session. "Where are you, Nancy? What are you seeing?"

I try to speak, but nothing comes out. Vaughn encourages me to speak,

"Can you describe what you are seeing?" I remained totally silent. I say nothing, and Vaughn asks me if it is okay to describe where I am…

The silence continued. I hear Vaughn, but I could not speak. Vaughn keeps trying, and I continue in silence. They will not allow me to speak.

Vaughn starts to speak of me being manipulated. I tell Vaughn there is a hand in front of me, and I ask, "Why won't they let me see? What is back there?"

I ask as I try to look around the hand they have placed in front of my face. Vaughn then asked, "What is the message that comes back?" "We are not ready," I replied. Vaughn asks "What is it that is keeping you from being ready?"

I say in return "They are not done." After another long silence I tell Vaughn that I was arguing with them in my head to stop this, and why they won't allow me to speak. I reassured Vaughn that they would never hurt me, and I continue telling him that they said they would always protect me.

"What are they protecting you from right now," Vaughn asks.

I tell him "harm." I continued to tell Vaughn they would never give me more than I could handle. Now, I find myself struggling to tell Vaughn "They are fighting you, Vaughn!" I apologize and tell him I don't want to hurt his feelings, and I did not want to tell him that. I continued "…for some reason they…"

Vaughn suddenly interjects, "I understand…" He continued to tell them that he was there for my higher good and he does not want me to go anywhere they do not want me to go during this regression. He continued, asserting that this "manipulation" needs to be dealt with. I am feeling very uncomfortable at this point.

I stammered as I said that it is a learning process for them, and that it is a need they must fulfill, and when I say "them," *they* remind me that includes *me*!

Vaughn asks if I am one of them. I do not respond. Vaughn then asks if they are "light beings."

I tell him they can be, and they can be whatever they have to be.

Vaughn probes further, "Are there any dark force entities that are interfering with your progress, Nancy?"

I answered, "Maybe you might see it that way, but I don't." Vaughn then asked to speak with the spirits and explains that he comes in the name of the Holy Spirit and the most loving energy, and that his interests are only in my healing.

I tell Vaughn I am asking them why I cannot be with them, and I am told that it has to be this way and that I will someday be with them. They told me that it might seem like a long time for me, but it was actually not.

Vaughn interjects again and asks them what my purpose here is, and I hear myself asking that question.

I tell him, "I am here to be exactly where I am, and doing exactly what I am doing." and then laugh because they tell me not to ask so many questions.

Vaughn stops my laughter immediately by asking about the baby. I tell him that there is indeed a baby, and there is more than one baby in the picture. Then seemingly as if I were no longer speaking, I communicated information that was so profound, it revealed a purpose for my collective contact experience:

Vaughn asks me "What is the purpose of the babies?"

I answer him "They are always striving for perfection."... divinity?

Vaughn questions. "What is the message for Nancy today that will benefit her the most?"

I said, "To understand that everything happens for a reason. Everything! To understand not to question, but to be a part."

Vaughn queries once again, "Why did they choose Nancy Tremaine?"

I tell Vaughn that I have always been with them.

Vaughn asks, "Are they willing to let go of the manipulatin...?"

I then immediately realized how much they dislike the use of the word "manipulation," and I answered quickly "No!" I told Vaughn they responded almost as fast as the word "manipulation" passed his lips.

Persistent, Vaughn continued "Is this manipulation in your best interest?"

Firmly, I replied that, "My best interest is their best interest!"

One more, Vaughn pushes on further asking "Are you at peace with that?"

Almost smugly I reply, "Yes, I am." Vaughn stopped asking questions, but I continued to answer his last question. "Many doors will be opening for me in the near future," I told him.

Vaughn again asked, "Are there going to be more babies?" I tell him, "There will be no more babies."

"Nancy," he asked, "will you then have an impact on their manipulation?" Once again, I feel the dislike they have over the word "manipulation" and I do not respond.

"Do they have your best interest?" he asks. "They need me and I need them, they have everything planned out, they have an absolute plan."

"Tell Nancy why she has had so much anxiety here on this Earth plane" Vaughn questions and I quickly reply, "Because I am not used to all of this…"

Then, my phone rang very loudly! This is the same phone I turn off at the beginning of each regression. I become startled, and one can visibly see my anxiety level rising.

I anxiously said to Vaughn "I turned off my phone! I turned it off – you saw me do it!" The phone rings loudly again.

You can hear my rapid breathing as Vaughn tries to calm me. I am almost in tears.

Vaughn tells me to understand that this anxiety is because of where I am.

I explain to Vaughn that the anxiety I am feeling is part of emotions I've never had to experience – all of the ugly emotions I was feeling right then were connected to this planet and the hatred in the world, the wars waged. These stir emotions that I and many other people aren't used to feeling with such intensity.

Vaughn asks, "What is the purpose of going through all of these deep emotions?"

"It's just part of the package," I say, "…to be here, and to experience."

"Is God behind these entities?" I tell him "God is the creator of all."

Vaughn continues, "Do you feel at peace from understanding?" I tell him "Yes, because I know I am not here for a long time."

Vaughn asked me to feel serenity and calmness. My breathing was deep and relaxed, and I felt as if I fell asleep. Vaughn asked me to connect these serene feelings with a word to describe them.

I told him "love." Vaughn assured me that everything is working as it was meant to. At this point, I was almost snoring, and I felt I was sleeping.

Vaughn asked me if there were any more questions I wanted answered, and I said to him I wanted to see the babies. He asked if I would be able to see them, and I respond with "They promised me I would see them."

Vaughn asked what the name of the baby was. I tell him that there is a boy and a girl. I named the boy "Drax."

Vaughn again asked me if there was anything else I wanted to communicate, and I tell him I want them to take me more and I want more messages and more answers – I want everything.

"Are they willing to do that," Vaughn asked, "Yes" I answer, "they promised they will." "Is there any unfinished business," Vaughn asked again.

"There is always unfinished business," I reply. Finally, Vaughn asks, "Are you satisfied with where you are at today?" I reassured him I am, and that I am grateful for all that has happened and all that will happen. I made it clear they were helping me.

Vaughn thanks them, and tells them they have nothing to fear from him.

I tell him lovingly, "They know that Vaughn." I was now in the deepest sleep I ever experienced. Vaughn assures me that I will get to see the baby soon. I reminded him of my daughter "Faylene…"

A Past Encounter

I quickly jumped ahead without any prompting and began to tell Vaughn of an encounter I had with Mr. when I was two or three years old. This was my earliest and surely one of my most frightening times with them.

I am shown a large rectangular cement pool or tank filled with water and divided into three sections. Each section contained a terrifying sea creature of some sort. Each creature lay silently on the bottom of their section, and had no room to swim, as there appeared to be only a few feet ahead of and behind them and the water they were submerged in was very deep, as the perception of light began to slowly fade with the ever-deepening water.

As I stood staring at them, I thought about how scary and ugly they looked. I failed to understand why they were showing me this, and didn't want to see them anymore. I was then instructed to choose one section and was told I would have to swim from one side of the tank to the other. I said with a trembling voice that I don't know how to swim, and I didn't want to do this.

I was then told, "You must pick one." I looked each one over. I was petrified with fear. One looked like a combination of a snake and an eel, and its body was in the shape of an "S."

Another was covered with scales and bumps, was fat and had whiskers on its face.

The last one appeared to be a giant goldfish all the way down to its orange color. Its texture appeared to be smooth. The other two creatures were just grey. I figured no matter which tank I chose to swim across, that I would be eaten. I finally decided on the tank with the orange creature in it.

Now, you, the reader, might ask yourself how a two or three-year-old would be able to recall such detail, and I would answer that query by stating when something this traumatic happens believe me, you remember.

Obviously, they did not require me to go through with this challenge, or I would not be here to tell you of my experiences! It was what I call a "fear challenge." Reptilians do not understand fear, and they do not experience feeling fearful.

Vaughn asked if it was to measure levels of fear, and I explained that even though they terrorized me I was in no danger. They were curious about which one I would choose; they wanted to know which creature I feared the least. I could tell Vaughn was feeling a bit unsettled.

He asked me if perhaps I might have felt manipulated. Little girl Nancy sighed, took a deep breath and said "Yeah...."

Vaughn then told me "You were a brave little girl! Do you understand at the deepest level? Do you understand just how brave you are?"

"Yes, yes I am," and then, I heard myself defending them again, explaining that this is how they learn. "Without fear you would never feel courage." I continued, "I'm supposed to help others not to be afraid."

Vaughn wanted to know if this was the lesson I was to learn, and I told him it was. Vaughn then reminded me about the young man I tried to help during the abductee meeting. I then realized that I was fulfilling my mission!

Vaughn asked if there were any other healing messages to share, and I told him with humor, "Enjoy the ride." That message has been given to me many times by the Reptilians working with me.

Vaughn then prayed for me. I assured him that this would all make sense someday. We are all watching the same movie. It is only that my screen is wider.

Three days after this final regression I was given this message:

"You were an abductee, then an experiencer, and now, you are a participant."

I sent this message to Vaughn along with the details of an incident in which manipulation of time took place. I also expressed concern that I was not normal. This is the email I received from him on May 28, 2012:

Nancy,

Your message in regards to being an abductee, then an experiencer and now a participant also defies space and time because the main message I was receiving during our last regression was that you have always been a participant. You are here on Earth to evolve spiritually through the intense levels of connectedness with the strong emotions of fear, anxiety, and love. You are alien by nature, human by choice, duty bound to improve your species or possibly even save them. You are an alpha and omega, both beginning and the end. Space and time appear to be necessary for us to hold our sense of self together for this learning opportunity. What's normal, anyway? I have no interest in being normal or sane. It is no good sign of mental health to be well adjusted to a profoundly sick society.

Vaughn Vowels

Chapter 7
Experiencing Time Manipulation, Drax, and Another Stay in the Hospital

"The apparent expansion of psychic or intuitive abilities, a heightened reverence to nature with the feeling of having a life-preserving mission, the collapse of space-time perception, a sense of entering other dimensions, realities or universes, a conviction of possessing a human/alien identity, a feeling of connection with all creation and related transpersonal experiences; all are such frequent features of the abduction phenomenon that I have come to feel that they are at least basic elements of the process..." **Dr. John Mack**

May 23, 2012: This was the very first day I was shown and allowed to experience the manipulation of time. I can only explain it as a feeling of being ahead of time or jumping forward in time, as if I have somehow fallen off the planet – unattached or no longer rooted in this plane. Sometimes it feels as if I am only a minute ahead of the rest of the world, and then there are other periods when it seems so much longer. I begin to feel less and less attached to this planet Earth.

I was on the highway, halfway through my ninety-minute drive to Sid's house. I've only driven there a few times since I prefer to be in my own home.

Sid makes the trip to my house twice a week, and stays with me three nights through the week. Any more would upset my need for privacy.

It was a beautiful sunny day and as always, my music was blaring and my entire body was keeping beat to the music. I took note that a car in the lane to my left was keeping pace with me. I figured it was just some guy checking me out and he would continue on his way if I just ignored him.

I realized however that he was not about to pass me until I acknowledged him. There was only a fleeting glance exchanged, but in those few seconds, a very strange connection took place. I could feel time slowing down such that I was able to make mental notes and remember clearly what was happening.

I knew I was about to experience something. The driver was a very handsome man that appeared to be in his late thirties to mid-forties. He had a head full of thick dark hair and wore black sunglasses.

I was wearing sunglasses as well, but still felt there was eye contact. He actually reminded me of the men in my family. It was much more than just a simple acknowledgement between a man and a woman, and it never felt like he was flirting with me but instead was trying to show or teach me something.

He gave me a slight smile as he pulled past me, and as the car passed me I could read the words "Trans-Am" on the right rear side of the car. I was compelled to remember every detail about what was happening now during this collapse of time. It was as if my mind was taking snapshots and they were being stored in memory.

I was no longer "in" the moment, but somehow "out" of the moment, and time no longer existed, or at least the movement of time was out of sync with the moment itself.

I have no knowledge of automobile makes or models, but this car stood out, and seemed quite unique. I thought to myself how odd this exchange between us felt, and I just knew he had been placed in my path.

Somehow I was made to understand that I would see him again. He sped up with a tremendous burst of speed and I felt the words "watch this" as he left my vision.

Within seconds I came upon an on ramp and I watched as a car merged in front of me. It was "him," the same man in the same red and black car. Again, I read the words "Trans-Am" as he zoomed ahead of me for the second time.

He wanted me to witness and understand the manipulation of time. There was absolutely no way this man could have gotten off the highway and then within seconds gotten back on to merge in front of me. Considering the highway, it was a sheer impossibility. I sped up after him, and I was determined to catch up to him. I wanted to get his license plate number, but couldn't even get close.

As the car up to 85 or 90 miles per hour, I realized the faster I went, the further away from me he would seem to go. My acceleration was propelling him forward at an identical rate of speed. It seemed that time did not exist.

During this whole event, I never saw another car on the highway. It was a mid-week afternoon on a busy highway, and I never noticed another car on the road. There are no words to explain what happened because there was so much more that took place during that event than words can express.

For the remainder of the drive my mind was completely preoccupied with this event. I couldn't wait to tell Sid about it. Alas, when I did, his response was as always – he didn't get it. For the next two days at Sid's house, I couldn't shake what had taken place. I replayed it over and over again in my mind.

When I got home, I wrote a letter to Vaughn telling him all about it. He found it fascinating as well.

It is June 12, 2012, and I am allowed to see my son Drax for the first time. I found myself aboard the ship and my daughter Faylene proceeds to hand me the bundle she holds, my son Drax.

Faylene is my hybrid daughter. I remembered nothing of her until my memories were returned to me after my third regression. I did remember a pregnancy – a real pregnancy in 1987, and even though I had a tubal ligation in 1978 and I knew it was just not feasible, here I was pregnant!

At the time I was living with a man, and I let him know. He insisted I take a pregnancy test. I didn't have to, however, because I knew I was pregnant. He was quite thrilled because he never had any children.

I on the other hand – was not. After I had my earth-bound daughter, I never wanted more children, never trusted that a man would stick around or support me.

One night as we lay in bed, we talked about the pregnancy, and he convinced me to take a pregnancy test the next day, just to be certain. I agreed to take the test. The following morning I was no longer pregnant and my stomach was again flat. There was no sign a baby had ever been growing inside of me.

Faylene, my hybrid daughter is beautiful. She is tall, slender, and appears to be human. Her hair is auburn, she has blue eyes, and just a few freckles spattered across her nose.

She was Drax's caretaker and I felt pleased that they were together. As she stood with Drax swaddled in a blanket, I noticed that his head was very large and misshapen. Although I could not see through the blanket, I could tell his body was very thin and frail and his back seemed to be somewhat hunched. I was appalled and disappointed.

He looked nothing like I had imagined he would look like. I felt betrayed. Faylene reached out to hand me the bundle she was holding and I backed away. I could feel her disappointment in me, and her deep sadness for Drax. I refused to make any eye contact with my son, because I knew he was telepathic and would be able to read my mind. Somehow, I just knew his eyes were blue. That was the final memory I had of being on board the ship.

I was so ashamed of myself. For days I would apologize, begging the Reptilians to please let me see my son again so we could bond. I promised to love and cherish him. Mr. then gave me this message: "Drax is exactly how he was meant to be. He is a loving and gentle being – he is a 'thinker.'" This word "thinker" describes a particular group of hybrids they are creating. The "thinkers" are just one of several groups of hybrids, and each group has a special purpose. I was told that Drax would make many wise decisions, as he is a "judge" of sorts, and that every society needs judges.

On July 4, 2012, Sid would see his first orb. We went to the annual fireworks display in Fowlerville where I lived. We took a blanket and got there early. This would be the first time we would watch fireworks together. As we lay on the blanket I looked up to the sky and noticed an orange orb with a glowing white light around it. The orb was quite a distance away and could have been blocked out with the tip of my finger.

I wanted to take a picture, but realized I would not be able to take a decent picture from that distance with my phone. I pointed it out to Sid, and he acknowledged that it was odd and like nothing he had ever seen before. He seemed intrigued with it, and for the next half hour or so, that is all he wanted to talk about. We could not take our eyes off of the orb as it drifted in a near perfect parallel line from one side of the sky to the next.

Each trip back and forth would take several minutes. I looked around where we were sitting, and no one noticed it at all. I wanted to call it to everyone's attention, but they were all speaking amongst themselves and anxiously waiting for the fireworks to begin.

All of the people there had children that were either playing on the swings or running around the park. After a while, Sid became bored watching the orb, but I never did. I never did. The fireworks began and everyone watched them contently except me.

I continued to watch the orb trying to imagine who was in this orb and what they were doing inside of it. I noted the time on my phone, and the orb was there for over an hour making a perfectly straight line across the sky, back and forth, back and forth.

Others must have seen this! I looked at everyone around me including Sid contently watching the fireworks, and I thought to myself, "There are none so blind...."

The next day, Sunday morning, Sid was seated at his kitchen table waiting for the breakfast I was preparing. I had both hands full as I went to place his plate in front of him and he asked me what was on my arm.

I looked down and saw a small red globule on my arm. I told him it was just raspberry preserves and asked him to remove it. He wiped it with his napkin.

As he did so, he got an odd look on his face and told me it was blood!

I sat the plates down and he examined my arm turning it in each direction. I asked him what he thought, and he said, "It looks like a claw mark..." I thought to myself that Drax must have been with me that night. I was pleased that Mr. had kept his promise and let me see Drax.

After breakfast, Sid and I had planned a two-hour motorcycle drive on his Harley, we would stop and have a nice lunch and just enjoy the beautiful day driving through the countryside.

I recall looking up to the sky hoping to see something. We stopped at a riding stable and inquired about possibly riding in the future. I knew that would never happen – Sid is afraid of horses. As a matter of fact, Sid is not fond of animals – any animal!

He said he wanted nothing to do with anything he would have to clean up after. In all the time I knew him, I never saw him once pet an animal. Even at friends' houses, if a pet approached him, he would avoid the poor thing and refuse to show any affection toward it.

I was always fascinated watching his reaction as a cat or a dog went out of its way to get his attention, and his ability to pretend it didn't exist. It always seemed odd.

One time I took care of my friend Tom's cat, "Cakies," while he and his girlfriend went on a cruise. Cakies was with me for a week, and when Sid came over he would actually take extra steps to avoid even going near her.

The one thing I like about cats is that if you don't like them, they will make your life miserable until you give in and acknowledge them. While Sid sat on the couch, the cat would sit in front of him – just staring. He was so uncomfortable.

I tried to encourage him to talk to the cat or just pet her. He never did. Cakies finally gave him a friendly, playful nibble on his foot. I witnessed this, and the cat didn't bite through his sock or even touch his skin, but he screamed like a little girl, shouting, "She bit me! That cat bit me!"

I pointed out that the poor cat had been trying to get his attention for hours and that she was just playing. Sid had to shut the bedroom door that night steeped in fear – of Cakies!

The cat knew it too, and the next morning she leaped onto the bed, landing on Sid's head. He was terrified and shrieked – there was also a lot of swearing as well. He kept screaming that Cakies had scratched him, but there wasn't the slightest mark. Cakies knew exactly what she was doing. Good for you, Cakies, I thought. Sid didn't come over again until Cakies was back at home with Tom.

When we finally returned home after our motorcycle ride I swung my leg around and over the seat only to find that the entire left side of my body was paralyzed. I had no use of my left arm or leg, and it literally scared the hell out of me.

I had never experienced anything like that. My entire left side seemed to hang off my body, and I had to drag my left leg on the sidewalk as I made it to the door. I thought, "Oh my God – I might have just had a stroke!"

Once inside, I could tell Sid was thinking the same thing. I lay on the couch and kept repeating the same thing – "I have absolutely no feeling, none!" It was as if someone made a perfect cut right down the middle of my body.

Sid suggested we go to the emergency room, and of course, I said, "No, absolutely not."

After a half hour or so, the feeling returned. I was relieved, but I realized it still might have been a stroke. I chose to try and forget all about it, but I could not avoid the fact that for the next several weeks I was stumbling, and it was difficult to get my feet off the ground when walking.

I was extremely dizzy, and my head felt as if it weighed 40 pounds. Sometimes my head would just fall forward and I would literally walk into a wall! I would frequently fall and my peripheral vision was somehow "off," not normal at all.

When exercising on my Pilates machine I fell off, and my entire back and butt were black and blue. It was so unlike me – I am usually very graceful walking, and I usually had terrific balance. I live in heels; I actually walk better in heels than I do in flat shoes. I can even run in heels! I wore high heels so frequently that my father once told a man I was dating that he would never get me to go golfing until they made high-heeled golf shoes.

On the first of August in 2013, Sid and I went to a popular art festival in Royal Oak, Michigan. There were amusement rides and live bands and art from all over the world, and booths full of delicious domestic and foreign foods.

We were only there for about an hour. We were standing up, listening to a band. I was having a wonderful time as Sid stood behind me with his arms around my waist.

Without any warning, my ears started to ring and I got extremely dizzy, and felt nauseous. I had to yell because the music was so loud, "I have to sit down Sid, because I am dizzy."

Sid held me as we quickly walked to an area less crowded. The next thing I recall was lying on the cement walkway – I passed out cold. Someone passing by carrying a folding chair offered it to Sid so I could sit down. Sid lifted me to my feet, and I passed out a second time. He told me I was out cold again for about 30 seconds.

I do recall coming to and asking Sid what happened. I was not able to sit up, and both of my arms were numb. A woman began pouring a bottle of water down my throat. I tried to help her, but my hands and fingers were numb and too weak to grasp the bottle. I kept looking for and asking for Sid.

The police had cornered Sid and were questioning him if I had anything to drink or if he had given me anything. The crowd gathered around me began to disperse, as the police were making room for the ambulance pulling up to where I was sitting. I thought to myself, "No way am I getting into that damn ambulance!"

I was certain the medics had a needle in there with my name on it. I felt bad that I ruined our wonderful day. I just wanted to rest for a couple of minutes so we could continue to enjoy the day.

A paramedic on the scene asked me how I was feeling and I told him I just needed a few minutes and I would be just fine. He told me I should consider going to the hospital, and that I had been out for quite a while. "It's just dehydration."

I assured him I had nothing to drink because I hate using those port-a-potties. It is a lifelong aversion. Even as a child, when we would vacation up north in a cabin with no internal plumbing, I would refuse to use the outhouse. I was terrified I would fall through and I could not breathe because of the smell.

My mother had a special pan for me so I never had to use that outhouse. As I write these words, I am thinking to myself, "She must have loved me a little to do that for me...."

The paramedic continued, "We cannot leave you until you stand up and show us you are okay." I thought to myself, "That's easy enough," and tried to use my arms to get up and realized I had no feeling from the waist down. I had no feeling, and there was no way I was going to stand up.

Sid stood watching and waiting for me to stand up, and I then motioned for him to bend down so I could whisper in his ear. I told him "I can't stand up, and I'm paralyzed. Just carry me back to the car." He told me he couldn't do that, we were parked two blocks away. Sid told the paramedics I could not move my legs, and I'm thinking to myself that Sid is a big tattle tale!

"No! No!" I kept saying as Sid gave the paramedics the nod, and I was loaded into the ambulance. As soon as I am inside the ambulance, out comes the "NEEDLE!"

They told me they had to start an IV. I am now hysterical, crying, screaming and fighting them. My legs were still paralyzed but my arms were working fine. I decided I would just continue to fight everyone off.

Sid is standing in the open doors at the back of the ambulance. "You are embarrassing me, Nancy, and you are acting terribly," Sid barked.

A female paramedic started reaching down my top to attach something. I pushed her away and growled back at her not to touch me. She then told the other paramedics that she had given up, "I'm not going to mess with her!"

After a few minutes of wrestling with the paramedics, they sternly made it clear that they were going to start an IV. I thought to myself they had better knock me out first. The administering paramedic made a deal with me and I accepted his offer. He said if I allowed him to place an IV into my arm I would not have to deal with any more needles when we got to the hospital.

"Please be gentle," I begged him. I then started to cry in agony as he inserted the needle.

They tell Sid to meet the ambulance at the hospital, and I shouted "Please! Run as fast as you can to the car! Go! Go quickly – please hurry!"

Sid never saw this side of me before because when I was in the hospital after the heart attack that never happened, I didn't even call him because I believed my life was over.

Now, here I am again just a few months later being quickly whisked inside yet another. I immediately feel fine and am no longer even dizzy. At the hospital I wiggled my toes and moved my legs – everything seemed to be in working order.

Why, I thought, hadn't everybody just left me alone like I asked in the beginning? I wouldn't be here! I looked up to see Sid walking toward me. The ambulance just barely beat Sid to the emergency room.

He looked very concerned, and I reassured him I was just fine and told him to, "Get me the hell out of here." A nurse came over to where I was and without saying a word, began tugging on the IV port in my arm.

"What are you doing," I screeched as I pulled my arm back and away from her. She told me she was removing the port in my arm.

"Oh, no you're not," I assured her in a stern tone of voice.

She explained that it was hospital policy that they place their own IV ports. I explained to her that the paramedic promised me I wouldn't have to go through this again.

"It's just hospital policy, she reiterated.

I brazenly told her, "This is simply not going to happen, and especially by you!"

She snapped back, "Then, we can't treat you here!" She was very aggravated with me and stormed off. I once again told Sid to "Get me the hell out of here!" Another angry nurse came over, removed the IV, and we were soon on our way back to my apartment.

Three days later on September 4th, I was still fainting and my heavy head was still running into walls. I passed out lying in bed. I was only in the hospital twice in my life: once to give birth at seventeen to my daughter, and the other for a kidney infection when I was nine. I am rarely sick, and I do not go to doctors.

Even for important women's issues, it has been over 20 years since I have had a pap smear. Finally, I gave in. Sid had been waiting for these words for a long time:

"You better take me to the hospital." With those very words we were in the car, driving to the same hospital I was admitted to seven months earlier. I realized there would be needles coming, and we discussed it all the way there. I figured it would be one needle for the IV port and I wouldn't have to be stuck again.

Concerned about going back there, I wondered what kind of a reception I would get. When we got there, the waiting room was packed, and it seemed like we waited forever. Because of that and a few other obvious reasons, I considered darting out the door and running!

When I finally was admitted, and after thirty minutes of refusal to cooperate and allow them to place an IV port, they gave me an

Ativan, medication used for people suffering from panic, and they were then able to place that IV. It also lowered my blood pressure, which was very high at 197/89. They said I was suffering with Transient Ischemic Attacks (TIAs), so they did medical tests to see if I suffered a stroke, they did a CAT Scan and an MRI of the brain, and an MRA of the neck.

Poor Sid spent nearly every minute of the two days I was admitted right by my side.

Strangely, I was experiencing hypersexual urges that seemed out of my control. Sid helped me with that problem, even though he protested "Nancy, we cannot do this here!" But we did. I was so wrapped up in these urges – I felt like Linda Blair in The Exorcist! What the hell was happening to me?

As it turns out, the MRI was negative for a stroke and after all these tests it was shown I had no abnormalities. That's pretty cool, right?

Even my cholesterol was perfect; they were not able to find even the slightest thing wrong with me. My physiology was spot on. Everything was well within normal limits. Now, ten months and two hospital stays have passed and I still have no answers. The physician who saw me at the hospital suggested strongly that I contact my family doctor and have an EEG and a sleep study done, just to rule out anything wrong associated with brain functioning.

I was still having problems with my hypersexual urges, and now, it seemed to be out of control, being constantly sexually aroused and insatiable.

While in the hospital, I saw several doctors and nurses and they all wanted me to explain what made me come to the hospital seven months ago. My response was always the same; my condition and what happened to me is in the medical records. That response never seemed to satisfy their curiosity. They would always ask me what condition it was and what had happened.

I would be made to use words that were highly sexually suggestive, such as "orgasm" and "ejaculation" over and over again. I believed they were all getting off just hearing me talk about it. Not one of them showed any concern nor offered any advice regarding what I was going through on a daily basis, and 24 hours a day, at that!

I made an appointment with my primary physician to schedule the EEG and the sleep study. I have to see my doctor every six months to get refills of my anxiety medication.

When I am in the office being seen I allow him to take my blood pressure and listen to my heart and lungs, nothing more than that. We discussed my two hospital visits and I mentioned that my "condition" was persisting and I needed answers. He too seemed surprised concerning what condition I was referring to.

I wondered to myself if they thought this condition was a "gift," and not a medical "condition." After I explained my "condition" using explicit language – the only real way to describe what's happening to me – I could see just how uncomfortable and embarrassed he was. He actually, physically, turned his back to me. With aggravated demeanor I scolded him; "Don't turn your back on me, this is a serious condition, and I need help!"

Everyone is too embarrassed to address the problem. He actually said in response to my assertiveness, "What do you want me to do about it?" I thought to myself – maybe grow a pair, doc. I shook my head in disgust and defeat.

He gave me the information for the sleep study and the doctor's name and phone to schedule the EEG, and I left the office. Sadly, in October of 2012 I broke it off with Sid. The relationship was proving to be unhealthy for the both of us. I continued suffering with my "condition," and ached for release constantly.

The sleep study was performed on November 29, 2012. I had high hopes this test would show something going on. I had no idea what it was they might find, but the hospital wanted to rule everything out.

I spoke with the woman performing the sleep study and asked her questions about the pineal gland. I finally quit talking and allowed her to hook my head up to the apparatus that measured my brain's activity. I finally did fall asleep, and in the morning, I was told – there was nothing wrong. My sleep patterns were normal.

Now, I had another appointment to attend with the doctor who was going to do my EEG. We discussed my two recent stays in the hospital. I explained to him that, although my head felt like cotton candy on the inside, on the outside it felt as if it weighed 40 pounds. I explained that my other "condition" was persisting, and I hoped that this EEG might hold an answer since everything else had been ruled out.

"What condition," he asked inquisitively.

"You know, my *condition*," I said with emphasis, "It's in the medical record."

"What is in the records," the doctor asked with some concern.

84

I said to him "You know – what happened."

"What happened?"

I said with some annoyance, "*It's in the records*!"

It started to feel as if we were performing an "Abbott and Costello" routine like "Who's On First?"

He told me there was nothing in the records about a "condition." He wanted to know what "condition" I thought he would find in the records.

I explained what was happening to me now. I was furious, and was thinking he was a pervert wanting me to talk dirty. He sat staring at me for what seemed like forever. So, I gave him the thrill I felt he was waiting for and fired off with those profane descriptive words – words I would never use in conversation!

Papers dropped from his hands along with his jaw! He appeared upset with me? He stood up and walked to the door. Not even looking back he said, "I'll have the front desk set up an appointment for you." He was gone!

The EEG was performed on December 3, 2012. The woman who administered the test was pretty young, so I thought she might be easier to talk to.

The first thing I asked her was if she had seen my medical records. She told me that she hadn't but that she was a technician and did not have access to the medical chart.

I told her about my in-bed and out-of-bed condition; she was curious at first, but then I lost her when I began going into detail. She said she had never heard of anything like I was describing to her.

My concern about my pineal gland came up and I asked her if this test might show some reason why this was happening to me. She told me that it might. I was hopeful. A few days later, I was anxious about the results and called the hospital only to find – the test was normal, absolutely normal.

Sid took me to Aruba for 5 days after all of this. This happened in December.

In February of 2013 I broke it off with Sid for a second time, although we would continue to get back together for sex. The cycle of break-up/make-up would continue for a period of several months until I found myself unable to even kiss him.

The sexual attraction was long gone. I didn't want him to touch me and he was aware of that. He was hopeful my feelings would return, however, I knew they would not. Our relationship truly went from hot to cold.

Backtracking a bit, before we left for Aruba I had called the hospital. I just had to know what the doctors and nurses had written in the chart. I wanted to understand why everyone seemed to go into "shock" whenever I mentioned "my condition".

A few days later the hospital records were ready, and I was more than excited to get my hands on them. I so desperately wanted to know what was in those records; I couldn't even get through the hospital doors.

Instead I deviated to the nearest waiting room, sat down and started reading. I didn't have to wait too long before I came across the words the two nurses in the first hospital wrote in the chart to describe my condition: "*She had a sex marathon.*"

I went into emotional overload. Tears filled my eyes. I felt ashamed, I felt dirty, I felt crazy, but mostly I felt betrayed.

The proper words, orgasm and ejaculation were never used to describe my condition. I went back to the records department with tears streaming down my face I said, "This is not true! This is a lie!"

Unconcerned, she just shrugged her shoulders and told me that it was out of her control. I went to my car and just sat and cried.

Sadness shortly thereafter turned into annoyance, and then annoyance into anger. I drove back to my home and called the hospital in order to get some much needed and overdue answers.

After making several phone calls to the hospital every day for over a week and asking them to please change my medical records to reflect what was actually happening to me, I finally received a letter from the patient relations department telling me the medical records would not be changed because they believed what the nurses had written in the records to be true.

After receiving that letter, I called the woman from the records department and told her that never, did I ever at any time use the words "sex marathon," and to inform her that those words were not a part of my vocabulary.

I explained to her how difficult it was for me to even come to the hospital and went on to explain to her my fear of doctors. I asked her if she really believed a sixty-two year old woman with post-traumatic stress disorder (PTSD) and a history of having been molested by a doctor would waltz into the emergency room proclaiming, "I just had a sex marathon!"

I went on to tell her that no nurse or doctor would ever be able to take me seriously once they came across those words. I wanted her to know that this condition I've had now for over a year-and-a-half makes it hard for me to get help. I'm telling every doctor and nurse what I am experiencing, and they are looking at me like I am crazy. I have nowhere to go, and no one seems willing to listen to me.

She then broke in and said, "You really sound upset. Have you thought of therapy?"

"Therapy?" I fired back, "Do you really think therapy is going to help me with this condition?" I realized I was not getting anywhere so I wrote the hospital the following letter to the female doctor that released me from the first hospital I went to:

August 26, 2013

…I know you have had many patients since me, but my condition was and is unique, and I am positive you remember me. You were the only doctor that treated me with any sense of dignity and respect besides Dr. Steele. I came to the emergency room because my heart would not stop racing and I feared I had a heart attack. This was extremely difficult as I suffer with PTSD and was previously molested by a gynecologist. I further stated to them I had experienced 30 or 40 orgasms and ejaculations. They chose to write instead that I had a sex marathon. I find that disgusting, and those words would never be a part of my vocabulary. These words will follow me for the rest of my life and will make it difficult if not impossible for anyone to ever take me seriously. Dr. Steele performed the heart catheterization and said there was absolutely nothing wrong with my heart. I was there for help, and I was treated like I was crazy. I need these medical records amended as you can only imagine the embarrassment these words will cause me as they follow me through life. What were these two nurses thinking? Now I realize why people were treating me so oddly when I mentioned my condition. The only condition they saw was a sex marathon. Since then, I continue to live with this condition, and it is now called PGAD, or Persistent Genital Arousal Disorder. It is rare and not pleasant to live with. I have tried to reach out to my primary physician, but he is too embarrassed to even discuss it. I don't think anyone understands or believes me, and this is frustrating. I am 63 years old now and it is putting a strain on my everyday life. I have since ended my relationship. I know you remember me because you were the first one to tell me it was probably a heart spasm. I responded I imagine that 30 plus orgasms and ejaculations would have killed a 20-year-old and you smiled uneasily and agreed with me. I know you will tell the truth and do the right thing. You have to live with this. I have researched all the information I can find, and I cannot locate one single woman of any age that has this condition or anything close to it....

I never heard back from that doctor or anyone from that hospital again. Out of desperation I did contact two attorneys. I never heard back from one of them and the other said they didn't handle such cases. No one believed it and no one wanted to hear it. The doctors, nurses and lawyers treated me as if I had told them aliens abducted me.

The one good thing is the medical records show I am in perfect physical condition. Retrospectively, I never imagined the pain I would experience writing this chapter and having to relive these horrible feelings.

I spoke of the Reptilians as being parents and teachers, and I stated I don't always like what they do. I realize now that all of the medical examinations I went through gave me solid evidence that I am in perfect health both physically and mentally. It was one of the many gifts "they" have given me, as they promised they would in my last regression with Vaughn. It was their gift of validation.

What humans have done to me is by far worse than anything the Reptilians or Mr. ever could. I am so relieved to put this chapter behind me. I am also learning who the real "bad guys" are.

Faylene Presenting Drax to Me

Chapter 8
Bonding, Missing Time, The Chief of Police and "Drax Tracks..."

"Is our reality a virtual reality game played by our higher selves for our enrichment or entertainment or is our existence manifested to entertain other higher life forms? Is there a higher life form that requires our essence as a nutrient for its well-being in the same manner we need to eat to survive?" Vasilios Gardiakos

October 4, 2012 was my 62nd birthday, and a birthday I proudly share with Dr. John Mack. We are exactly twenty years apart to the day. My birthday present from Mr. would come 6 days later on October 10th.

It was a little past one o'clock in the afternoon and I was putting some makeup on. I don't recall if I had planned to go anywhere but it is never unusual at any time for me to be putting on makeup.

I am a girly-girl, and love all that entails. I caught a glimpse of what appeared to be red scratches on the left side of my chest atop my breast. I wanted to get a better look, went to the large mirror in the dining room and could not believe what I was looking at!

There were two very red and very raised infected-looking scratches. Upon closer look, I noted a starting point where a small red circular bump was located in front of each scratch. I placed my right index finger very gently on the top scratch to feel the raised bump. I was expecting to say "Ouch!"

Strangely, however, there was no pain – no feeling! I skimmed my finger across the entire length of the top scratch. Not only did it *not* hurt, but also I could not feel a raise in the skin. It was flat to the touch.

I began to rub my index and middle fingers across the entire surface of the scratches. It was as if they did not exist! It was like there was nothing there. These raised, infected-looking scratches were a hologram. I thought, "How can this be possible?" My right arm brushed across my right nipple, and that hurt like hell! My nipple felt as if it had been put in a vice. It looked normal, and it wasn't red or discolored.

I scrambled for my phone, and was shaking and jumping around like I usually do when I get over-excited. I was shouting, "Oh my God! What the hell is going on? Oh my God! Oh my God!" I could hardly push the numbers to call Harry.

I listened to his phone ring, all the while whispering under my breath, "Come on, Harry... pick up the phone... Pick up the phone!" and before he could even say hello, I frantically began telling him what had happened.

"Harry, Harry – you're not going to believe it..." I went on to describe the bright red infected looking scratches that were not really there, and that there was no feeling to them, and that my right nipple was in pain, but it appeared to be absolutely normal.

I was still excited, still invoking God over and over. I was practically running in place. Harry said, "Get pictures! Get pictures now, because those marks are going to fade quickly."

He sounded a bit wound up as well. I wondered how and why he seemed to know that the marks would fade quickly. I then realized how important this was. I had something of *great* importance, so with each picture I took, I shouted, "I got ya! I got ya!"

I took picture after picture and as I did, I could see the marks start to fade. In about four hours the scratches were all but gone. Only light pink marks the camera could barely detect remained. They were almost completely gone by the next morning. I made sure to send the pictures to both of my e-mails, because I didn't want to lose them and couldn't wait to share them.

Sadly, there were only a handful of people I could share with, including Harry and Vaughn, one family member, and the State Director of MUFON. My cousin Chris had been a constant supporter in this process.

Every time I would say I want to quit, or that I was done with the whole thing, he would tell me I had an important story to tell, and he would encourage me to carry on. There were times I knew he was very busy, but he would always take a few minutes out of his day to talk to me. He was always on my side. Thank you, Chris!

Of course I called Sid, and he came over the following day to find nothing more than faint pink marks. I asked Mr. (through telepathy) what was happening to me. The answer came in the form of a mental image and I was compelled to draw it.

It is included in my many illustrations. Drawing has been a form of communication between the Reptilians and me. I saw myself holding Drax as he nursed from my right breast as his small, clawed hand clutched my left breast. They had kept their promise and allowed me to bond with my son! I wondered if there had been other times they did not allow me to remember. Drax was now nearly six months old. In the future, Mr. would continue to give me validation in the form of physical proof.

On October 11, 2012, the day after the scratches, I sent this e-mail to Harry:

> "...I just got off the phone with Landi, and she too did not feel this was done with malice and believed it was my son nursing. I'm sure Drax did not mean to scratch me. I know this sounds funny, but I don't want the marks to leave me because I feel more bonded to him than ever! I don't fear anything that is happening to me. I feel I am becoming more and more connected with them. I feel very fortunate. Sound crazy? Welcome to my world, Harry..."

Little did I know just how strange my world would become. I had become part of something I did not fully understand, but I welcomed it and was thrilled to be a part of it.

On October 30, 2012, I awoke as they floated me back to my bed and gently placed me on my back. I was being returned, and was catching them in the act. They wanted me to feel comfortable with their presence and to never feel fear.

They reminded me of a message they had given to me: I am not to question, but to be a part of. As they left I began to choke and gag. I sat straight up and a warm fluid ran down my face and chest.

I turned on the lamp next to my bed and was immediately met with bright red blood spewing from my left nostril. I gagged on the taste of blood, spitting it from my mouth. As I ran to the bathroom I tried to catch the blood gushing from my nose with both hands.

The bleeding stopped within a minute, as it was just another day in my life. I am not prone to bloody noses, and the only other one I remembered getting was on May 9, 2012, the day after my fifth and final regression and two days prior to my receiving a message from Mr. telling me I was now a participant.

I had no proof of the Novi, Michigan incident, sadly. I wanted to start keeping records and data concerning my experiences. Retired Chief of Police, Lee BeGole made a phone call to me in October of 2011 regarding the 1961 incident, and I missed an opportunity to make a record of our calls. To remedy this, I purchased a tape recorder and have recorded every phone conversation between the Chief and I for the past three years. I did not record the dates of each particular call, so I wasn't sure of their order.

However, I have two recorders with four files each, and his health and memory varied from call to call, so some are clearer and cogent, while others reflected his medical as well as his mental status. Lee BeGole, Novi Chief of Police, was ninety-one when we first spoke.

I guess I recorded those calls more for my sanity and validation than for any other reason. I made many calls to the Chief over the years, and most went unanswered despite leaving messages. Later I would find that the Chief was in the hospital or had been too ill to respond.

Lee BeGole started working in the Novi, Michigan police department in 1954. He was the very first police officer. He was also the very first Chief of Police, and sometimes, he was also the Novi Fire Chief. The Novi Police Department is one of the finest in the state.

By 1955, they acquired their first two-way radio system and in 1958 Novi Township was the largest incorporated village, and the police department had grown to seven officers strong.

It was Lee BeGole who instituted many of the high standards currently upheld by the Novi Police Department. If one wanted to be considered as an applicant to the department, one must be a veteran of the armed forces with an honorable discharge. Novi was also the first police department that required all officers to have a four-year degree.

To be sure, these high standards were a reflection of the personal integrity and high moral values to which BeGole conducted himself his entire life. BeGole graduated from the University of Western Ontario with a pre-law degree and in 1952 he graduated from the University of Detroit, School of Law and subsequently passed the Michigan bar exam. Thus, when Lee BeGole retired in 1991, it marked fifty years of selfless service to his country, his city, and its citizens.

I called Chief BeGole in 2012 and below you will find excerpts from our third conversation.

BeGole said, "I do remember very well being there that night. I also remember that the first time we spoke I had a pretty good memory but something has happened that caused that to die." I thought to myself, "Oh my God, he's had a stroke!"

BeGole continued, I can't remember the incident, but I remember the dates..." He said "dates," which was plural. This is still to this day puzzling to me.

I was mentally kicking myself in the ass for not recording that first phone call I made to him. He told me that he remembers Officer Martin Cone calling him on the two-way radio and stating "...strange object overhead," and BeGole said he thought to himself, "Now what is wrong with him?"

He spoke of the city councilman's wife, Mrs. Young calling. He promised to work on his memory and told me he appreciates my keeping after him, and he urges me to continue to keep calling him.

I said to him, "I just cannot let it go." And he told me, "Don't let it go! You have a very deep interest in this, and I want to work with you."

I told him just how traumatic it was for me, as I was just a child. He stated, "I do remember it – that's the big thing."

He quickly defended the department and himself, "We did take action. We sent the cars out. One of the calls we got was from one of our patrol cars, and I even went out to the scene afterwards, to the Meadowbrook Lake Subdivision. Martin Cone moved to North Carolina, and the last time I heard from him was about five years ago. I know he would remember this, but I don't know how to contact him."

I am then reminded of a conversation with my girlfriend Cindy who told me that BeGole was at her home that night talking with her father. A flash of memory returned to me. I recalled my mother asking my father if he thought they should take me to the hospital, and my father responding "And what do we tell them, Jackie?"

I wanted to ask BeGole many more questions. I knew I would have to "spoon feed" him so as to not frighten him away. There would be months of me leaving messages on his answering machine with no return call.

I cannot remember how many times I said to myself, "That is the last damn phone call I'm making to that man!" But, it never was. I believed that, like my parents did, BeGole wished I had forgotten that evening back in 1961, and the need to find answers.

I made several trips to the Novi library and spoke with several employees, and was even given access to the archives, which I methodically searched through. I spent hours going day by day, page by page. I only looked at the first two pages of each issue because if it were in the Novi News, it would certainly be "front page" news.

Novi was a small village back then; there was not much to report. I finally received a call from a librarian telling me that she had tried to find information regarding the event and was unable to come up with any information.

She also told me that the Novi historian had no knowledge of the event. She went on to tell me that the Novi historian didn't even live in Novi back then!

I felt as if I reached another dead end. I did, however get the names of three more Novi police officers that were on the force in 1961. I now had the names of five out of the seven original Novi policemen. Attempting to track them, their families or relatives led me to another frustrating dead end.

For most of December, 2012, something odd would happen to my car maybe once or twice a week. It did not matter where I parked my car, it didn't matter what time of day it was.

There would be gigantic water beads on my car (I have video proof). The beads were only on the roof, hood and trunk of the car. The sides, undercarriage and the ground underneath and around the car would be dry. The beads appeared to have been blown on the car by a big wind, as they always seemed to be aligned in the same direction.

I would walk around the parking lot or wherever I was parked, and found there were no other cars with beads of water – not even wet! My car was the only one affected in this way.

At first, I tried to ignore it. But the second and the third time it happened it finally got my attention. I kept telling Sid about it but he seemed totally disinterested in it until one day he was going to his car to get something and came rushing right back in.

"What the fuck is up with your car?" Aha! I have been telling everyone about this and no one seemed to think it was a big deal.

"Well," I said, "Now you see it! You wouldn't listen to me. Nope! You wouldn't listen. Well, there it is!" I asked him what he thought it was.

"I don't know," he said. And that was the extent of his concern.

I decided to ignore the big water drops that only appeared on my car. After I decided to ignore this phenomenon, it stopped. It was very strange. I sent the videos of the car to a former MUFON investigator (retired from his position for twelve years).

He responded by telling me that the drops were unusually large and didn't look right. He said it was almost like the car sweated the water out of the metal. That is very strange, but it's the kind of validation they leave. Whatever it was, it had to have been manifested from above the vehicle.

In January of 2013, Sid and I were invited to stay at my friends Greg and Ron's house in Illinois for a couple of days. Greg and I have been good friends for over 25 years and we have seen each other through a lot of difficult times, and much of it I prefer to forget.

Greg has always been a bit of a bully, but his good qualities outweigh the taunting and teasing he put me through. He also had a way of bringing up the most embarrassing things I ever did and sharing these personal things with friends and family.

I asked him many times not to do this, but for some reason he just didn't understand, and this behavior just continued. We met in the late 1980s when we worked together in a small restaurant. He was a short-order cook and I was a waitress. When I refused to serve nachos whose tips were often burned black to customers, the owner would make him redo the order.

The looks I got from him were not pleasant. Our personalities were not well matched, and it seemed that we would never become friends, but we ended up bonding one afternoon at work. That day we followed the sounds of moaning and mumbling coming from the dishwashing area in the back of the restaurant.

We were quite surprised to find the dishwasher with his mouth hanging open as he frantically pointed to his jaw trying to speak. He was just a teenager. We laughed our asses off not realizing the seriousness of his condition. This went on quite often and this poor kid would have to manually manipulate his jaw back into alignment with his skull.

He ended up in the hospital, and they had to break his jaw to reset it. When I went to the hospital to visit him, I could see that he was in a lot of pain. This was certainly not a minor surgical procedure! After this, Greg and I became close friends. We would occasionally go to Las Vegas together. Greg is only a few years older than my daughter and he is gay.

He is also the only friend of mine that did not make Sid feel threatened. Greg and his partner Ron have lived together for years and they adopted Rob's niece who has a learning disability. She lived with them from the age of fourteen until she was twenty-one. She now lives in a group home and is thriving.

Sid and I looked forward to our stay at their beautiful home. We had only been at their home for a few hours and were seated for a fantastic dinner they had prepared for us.

We were still eating the salad when I bit down and one of my front teeth broke off and landed in my salad. I dug through the lettuce and found my tooth. I was very upset and ran straight to the bathroom mirror and started crying.

It is amazing how much different a front tooth can make in a person's appearance. My trip was ruined. I not only had a missing front tooth, but I also realized to replace it was going to cost well over two thousand dollars that I did not have. It broke off at the root. Everyone thought it was hilarious; Ron was the only one not laughing and joking because he understood how important my appearance is to me. I take great pride in my figure, how I look and dress. I have always been fastidious about appearances. Sid and Greg seemed to think it was no big deal, and encouraged me to return to my dinner. I did not want to ruin the dinner for everyone, so I made my way back to the table to find Grant with a piece of food blocking one of his front teeth smiling. I began to cry harder, and expressed with anger, I did not find this funny. I grabbed Sid's hand and pleaded with him to ask Grant to stop. All I got in return was an empty stare. Greg said I looked like a toothless hillbilly and Sid roared with laughter. This went on for the entire two days we were there.

Either they were telling me what nutcases ufologists and MUFON members were or they would ask me how my tooth was doing. Sid lacked in leadership and was easily led by Greg. I could not wait to get home! I was simply tired of this childish behavior. I quickly got tired of attempting to change the subject when my tooth or Ufology became the topic of conversation. Greg's partner Ron even jumped in defending me and telling them both I had enough. When a person sees their behavior is hurting the other, they usually quit. I was tired of the words "alien" and "flying saucer" being thrown around. When the laughter subsided, I made it clear to all that this was exactly why I kept my mouth shut for fifty years. Sid knew to keep to his side of the bed that night.

Greg had always teased me and I was always able to handle it. However, since 2013, when I shared my regressions and the 1961 event with him, our relationship forever changed.

He refused to even look at any of my videos and it was all I could do to force him to look at any of my illustrations. He found them amusing and ignored me if I tried to talk to him about it.

Ron, on the other hand, was very interested and asked lots of questions and was intrigued with my illustrations, and this seemed to bother Greg. I never understood why and I questioned if Greg doubted my honesty. He had seen all my faults, but lying has never been one.

Once we got home I sent Sid on his way and locked myself in for several days. I felt worn down and exhausted. I had become physically ill over it all, and this was not the first time this has happened. I needed to recharge. Sid repeatedly apologized and "kissed ass," even giving me money for the cost of my broken tooth which now sports a crown. My need for sexual relief would allow Sid back into my home.

There were times I could feel the energy of Mr. enter me and I knew he was able to experience my sexual pleasure. Sid was able to sense this at times, and would remark "Mr. really enjoyed that..." Sid had become nothing more than a vessel. Mr. gave me this message during lovemaking: "It is much more difficult to manipulate thought and emotion than the physical."

I talked with Cindy several times about this event and we were able to have some very good conversations when she was sober enough to recall and discuss that day in 1961. She remembered I was missing and that it seemed like a long time. That memory never changed or faded. She recalled our fathers were together and that they were both worried. Every time she would say, "You were gone," I could only try to imagine the panic my father must have felt. He always needed to be in control, so that explains much of our relationship after that. When I was not grounded, dad had to know where I was every second, so it seemed. Cindy also mentioned how the word in Novi was that the government had come in and "cleaned house."

I found it really odd that Cindy mentioned a small lake between our homes – all the locals called it "Man Made Lake" – and she believed the ship came and went from that body of water. I thought the same thing but never mentioned it. Even Chief BeGole spoke of Man Made Lake! It's really odd that Cindy, just like me, never watched an episode of Star Trek, Lost in Space, or any other science fiction show.

"Why would I not watch those shows," she questioned me, and

I told her for the same reason I did not watch them. They were fake!

Cindy kept saying, "Maybe it was just a dream, but I remembered being in this tube, and they were on the outside. I watched as they did things to you."

I asked her to describe them, and she got very upset. "Oh, they were awful," she sighed, "They looked like big frogs. And those eyes, those big eyes!"

She again mentioned that it might have been a dream she had. I explained to her that was normal, and I felt that way too at times. She also told me they told her they would not hurt me nor would they hurt her. She said when she left me on board the craft she did not worry because she truly believed they would not hurt me. I even drew an illustration of Cindy in this clear, plastic-looking tube:

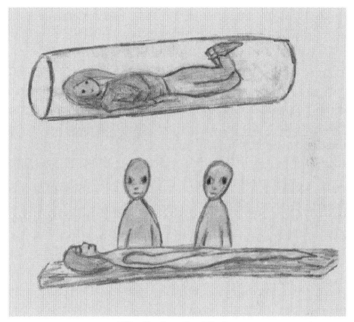

Cindy in the Tube

Why would Cindy keep telling me over and over that she had her clothes on? She would only be prompted to say that if she saw me on board the craft without clothes on!

I apologized for her having been brought on board, as I knew they did it to appease me. I just would not stop screaming at them, "I want Cindy, I want Cindy! I don't want to be alone!" I was screaming that as I was running away and just before they shot that electrical device that froze me in my tracks.

It is January 27, 2013. Roy has been one of my best friends for several years. He has met many of my family members and has even done business with my friend Tom.

Most of my friends have been men as I feel most comfortable with them. Another strange coincidence here is that Harry was one of Roy's teachers.

It was months after I met Harry that he would make that connection. Roy comes over once a week or so. We enjoy each other's company, and I can talk to him about anything. He is a calming force, like a tranquilizer to me. He is very laid back and has his emotions well in check, very much like my friend Tom.

I need people like this around me because I am so overly emotional and high-strung. Of late, Roy has become very interested in Ufology and all of my experiences. He has never doubted me and has always been supportive. I don't recall what movie we watched that night, but Roy was plagued with the "heebie jeebies."

His shoulders would rise and fall, all the while making the noises one would make when they are watching a horror movie. Several times he mentioned that the hair stood up on the back of his neck and his arms. He swears he saw electrical sparks coming off of me. He even mentioned this to Harry.

At the time it did feel odd, and we kept looking around as if we were expecting something to happen. Well, the mystery would be solved the next morning,

On January 28th, I slept in as is usual until about eleven o'clock in the morning. I made my way to the kitchen with eyes half opened and acquired my morning cup of coffee.

I warn people – don't talk to me in the morning! Don't even look at me! I hate mornings, and I am useless until I've had my first cup of coffee. Grabbing my cup of coffee I headed toward my living room.

As I pulled back the curtain, I was met by a set of tracks clearly leading from my patio to a fenced area located well off the property. It had snowed the day before, and today the weather was much warmer and you could see that these tracks were starting to melt. They appeared in a nearly straight line, and seemed to run as far as the eye could see. I opened the patio doors and stepped out to get a closer look.

As I bent down to inspect them, I noticed that they veered off the side of the patio and made a line directly to my bedroom window. Below, the photos show the tracks that Drax made in the snow:

"Drax Tracks"

"Drax Tracks" to My Bedroom Window

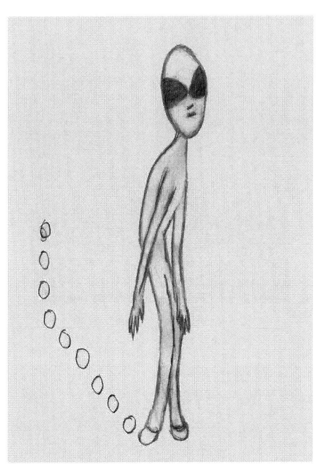

Drax Making Tracks in the Snow

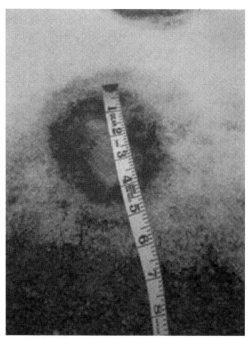

"Drax Tracks" Measurement

There were no other footprints anywhere in anyone else's yard. The tracks were the only ones visible. I was puzzled to say the least, and went back in to grab my camera and started to take pictures, and even some video.

I even pulled out my tape measure. The tracks measured about three inches or so in length, and there was only about three inches between each step. I knew nothing about animal footprints, but knew these tracks were not made by an animal, but by what appeared to be a "horseshoe" shaped device only totally circular – very strange indeed.

I called Roy who was over just the night before to come over and examine the tracks. Roy is a farmer, a retired Air Force veteran and a former fireman. He is serious no-nonsense person. He assessed the tracks. He said, "These were not made by an animal. I've never seen tracks like these before." He mentioned how eerie it was that they led right up to my bedroom window, and also commented on the small size of the tracks. Little did Roy know it, but he was being pulled into this "high-strangeness" and had now become a big part of it. We both understood why last night felt so very odd to us. Neither of us could even guess how the tracks got there. This event we shared strengthened our friendship and alliance as we both shared something most people would not understand – we did not understand it! My friendship with Roy caused Sid a great deal of jealousy and distress. According to Sid, anything that didn't involve him was a threat to our relationship. After this experience, Roy and I would frequently get together to do research and watch DVDs on abduction and shows I recorded about Ufology. As of this writing, we still share stories and shake our heads in bewilderment as one thing after another occurs on this wild roller coaster ride.

I was invited to attend a few meetings for abductees which brought me comfort. During one of our meetings I showed the videos of the tracks and the scratches on my chest to the members. No one had ever seen anything like them, and to this day no one, except me, has an answer as to what they are. I remember exactly where I was and what I was doing when I would learn what those tracks were. I was in my kitchen looking at my calendar and heard the voice of whom I knew to be my hybrid son, exclaim, "Drax tracks! Drax tracks!"

It all made sense now, indeed if any of this makes sense! "Yes, Yes!" I would repeat over and over again as I stood in my kitchen crying, then laughing, and crying again.

I was then given a mental image of Drax who was then nine months old making his way to my bedroom wearing snow boots on his feet with metal horseshoe like devices attached to the bottom of the boots as he walked through the snow. I am curious if anyone is familiar with these horseshoe-type boots, and I wonder if this might be something aliens wear to walk in snow.

It sure makes sense. My son Drax is a "digitigrade," meaning he walks on his toes with his heels off the ground. I thought to myself they could have easily dropped him off to be with me, but then I wouldn't have the validation that they were giving me a gift.

In my last regression I told Vaughn that they were giving me gifts. They could have also given him a different name but then it would not have rhymed with "tracks." I laughed at their sense of humor and how difficult it is for me to try and explain this stuff to people. I thought, "Drax tracks!" Thank you, Mr., and thank you, Drax, for more validation and proof by way of pictures and video.

I couldn't make this crap up! I don't think anyone could! There are no cables or wires running the length of my yard, and absolutely no way those tracks would have been made artificially. In the pictures and videos, the viewer can clearly see there is not another mark anywhere else in the snow.

The back of my complex was clean untouched bed of snow with one line of tracks coming across the property toward the patio and then veering off toward my bedroom window. I have been asked if the tracks were coming or going, and I always say coming, because that is the mental image I was given of my son making his way through the snow. How precious he looked. Today I challenge anyone to try and reproduce those tracks in the snow.

On February 21, 2013, Roy was over for what I believe was the first time since the tracks were found. We had just watched an episode of "Ancient Aliens" that I had recorded.

It was around ten-thirty in the evening and being a farmer Roy never stays too late. The day starts early for him at about four or five o'clock in the morning. I walked into the kitchen to get some water and happened to notice the time on the microwave clock. It reported one-thirty in the morning! I said to Roy, "It is one thirty in the morning!" Roy chuckled at that statement. I said emphatically, "No, it really is!"

"Well, that can't be right," he replied, "It was just ten-thirty." We checked our phones and the time on the television and yes, it was one-thirty in the morning!

Roy said, "I don't understand. What happened? We were just sitting here, right?" He was asking me for confirmation. I reassured him, "Yes. Neither of us has moved. We have been sitting right here."

Roy's face was shrouded in absolute disbelief as I realized we had just experienced three hours of missing time. He couldn't comprehend what happened and neither could I, as that was the first time I recalled experiencing missing time.

On February 24th I sent a letter to the State Director of Michigan MUFON along with pictures and videos of the tracks. In the letter I told him,

"The main reason I am writing to you is because there has been a lot of extraterrestrial activity going on in my life. It seems to be going very quickly now, and I seem to be running ahead of time. I think you understand what that means. I have videos and pictures I am willing to share. I also have a friend who has been witness to things going on. I have known him for several years and he is very credible, an ex-firefighter and retired from the Air Force, and he is a farmer by trade. He is very laid back, quiet, and not one to show much emotion. He cannot believe what he is seeing and experiencing. I am keeping a log of everything. I used to get excited when something

105

happened, but now I just find myself exhausted from all of the frustration and isolation. I think they are actually numbing me, or making me immune to all of this activity."

On March 6, 2013 I once again contacted MUFON telling them we really needed to talk.

In the email I told them,

"I took several videos of the tracks. Did you see the pictures with the measuring tape? Those tracks are three and a half inches across and one and a half inches deep. They were only three inches apart and in a near perfect line. They were circular, and you could clearly see the cutout in the middle. I did not go back to where they led to, and I don't know why. I guess I was in shock after taking the 6 videos. I have more to share, so much more! I have a very credible witness as well. He was visiting me the night the tracks were made. He kept telling me the hairs on his arms were standing up and he watched as electricity sparked off my body. We also had around three hours of missing time. He would gladly speak with you. There is no animal that could have made those tracks, and they are only going one way. Those tracks are unexplainable by anyone. I have more to share than can be done by a phone call. Things are going very fast. I want to get my videos out to see if someone can explain them. I have received a message telling me exactly what they are. I just got off the phone with Harry, and he is excited by all of this, too."

His reply came the same day. He thanked me for sharing and said it was fantastic that I had recorded it. He said nothing, however, about speaking with Roy or sending an investigator out.

I thought, with a hybrid child, claw marks, tracks in the snow and missing time there would be a lot to investigate, not to mention the many messages I had received as well as numerous hospital visits. I informed him about all of these things, and I happen to know that MUFON in many other states come to investigate much less. I listened to speakers at our MUFON get-togethers that had literally put people to sleep. I knew I had important information to share.

On March 13th again I reached out to MUFON. The director's wife had recently given birth, and I figured he and his wife might be preoccupied with the new baby's care.

I wrote,

"I understand that with the new baby and work you must be on overload. I have accumulated so much more information than I could share over the phone. Maybe you could give my email address to David Twichell that does all the videography for the MUFON meetings in Michigan. Please give him my number and see if he has a time that he could meet with me if he is interested."

Well, I never heard from him. By this point I was frantic and unable to sleep at night, I was very anxious and *very* frustrated. I cried a lot. Harry did not understand what the problem was (with MUFON) either.

Harry told me it had been years since he was involved with MUFON and perhaps they handle things differently. Handled things differently I thought… They just didn't handle things at all.

On March 24th I finally got the state director to give me some time to show and tell my story. I was chomping at the bit – I couldn't wait to get started. I was told to arrive a half an hour early. I personally invited two women I had met through the abductees group to come and meet me there.

The state director watched my videos and looked at my pictures. I expected the investigators and the videographer might also be present, and was surprised that the only other people attending were the two women I invited.

Afterward, several people asked me what I was showing to the small group in the corner. When I told them what I was showing, they were all very disappointed they had not been told and none of them could understand why they had not been given the chance to see my presentation.

I was confused as well. I carried my illustrations with me to nearly every presentation I attended and eagerly shared them. Everyone there was interested in my story except the State Director. After the current speaker was finished I spoke with one of the MUFON investigators who just happened to be sitting at the same table as I was, and I opened up to him.

I found myself pouring out to this man. He too felt left out missing my presentation. I felt as if I was going to lose my mind unless someone decided to *listen* to me and take my story seriously. I prayed this investigator would take an interest and help me figure this ongoing and baffling situation – as I was further drawn into being a part of the plan Mr. had for me.

He seemed extremely interested in my story and asked for my phone number and email address. He got back to me after a couple of days. I knew I had piqued his interest!

I had only attended a few MUFON meetings, but was comfortable with familiar faces at each presentation. I, along with many MUFON attendees, received an email inviting us to have dinner with David MacDonald, the international director of MUFON at the time, because *none* of the investigators were able to attend.

Now, I saw this as a great opportunity to share, but during the gathering it was unfortunate the time never seemed right and there were too many conversations going on at the same time for me to feel comfortable enough to open up. This was a pleasurable get together, and I guess business was going to have to wait. I left the dinner feeling even emptier than when I arrived.

I felt so alone and only had my tape recorder to share with. Today, when I listen to myself on those tapes, it breaks my heart. On the tape I am crying and barely able to speak, these are my words, "I feel like I am drowning and I am reaching out my hand for someone to take it. I keep reaching out to people and no one reaches back. I think I'm going to lose control – it's all too much. I am all alone and I feel isolated. It seems no one can understand what I am going through because there isn't another sixty-two year old woman with a hybrid child. I cannot even talk about the sexual aspect because it makes people uncomfortable. I can't even talk with my fucking family doctor because he is too embarrassed, so here I am alone, isolated, drowning. I am begging for someone to reach out and say, 'I will help you.'"

Sid and I had been invited to Orlando to stay with Greg and Ron from March 23 to April 1, 2013. Their adopted niece and her boyfriend were staying there also.

It was a huge condo and we would be given the upstairs bedroom and bathroom, and it afforded us complete privacy. It really was lovely. I had some reservations about going. I remembered how Sid and Greg treated me during our Chicago visit.

Sid had just shared a troubling story with me regarding an ex-girlfriend and her two children and their vacation in Florida. He laughed as he explained how he had left them all there in Florida and went back to Michigan by himself because her children did not like the activities he had planned for them.

I was not bringing any children, and the thought of getting out of Michigan and seeing the Florida sunshine won out! Well, the weather in Florida was terrible most of the trip and even with a jacket I froze.

Also, Ron was extremely ill and I only was able to see him a couple of times as he spent all of our time there in bed. Greg told me he had to meet a deadline on a project at work, so Sid and I took the kids with us every day.

Sid turned into a different person as soon as we arrived. It was like he and Greg fed off of each other. I was again made the butt of every joke and again, MUFON was referred to as "The Cult of the Crazy."

I ignored them this time, but it seemed to fuel the flames. I would go upstairs and watch television or do crossword puzzles refusing to allow this treatment to affect me.

One night Greg and Sid had too much to drink and they started with the "alien shit" again. I looked at Sid and said, "What about Drax?" Sid responded in his drunken demeanor, "Who is Drax?" My blood pressure was peaking. I asked him to explain the tracks leading to my window and the wet car. He said through his drunkenness, "I don't know what you're talking about." He was looking at me right in the eyes with such satisfaction.

I have never hit a man, but I had the powerful urge to whack him upside the head. It was my own fault, and I take full responsibility for allowing them to get me so riled up I thought it necessary to defend myself.

I should have ignored them, acted as childish as they did by even entertaining them. I headed upstairs and gave Sid that look that clearly said, "You know what you did, and it's over." Sid came upstairs about an hour or so later and I was in bed for the night watching TV. Sid was drunk, and he kept apologizing to me and trying to have sex with me. He reeked of alcohol and was a disgusting mess.

When I refused, he became irate and continued trying. My voice boomed as I shouted "NO!"

Well, Sid was furious and started packing his things and yelling, "I am out of here, and you can find your own way home." As he said those words, an energy entered the room causing the whole room to vibrate. Sid jumped into the air!

He was terrified and looked straight at me as he screamed, "What was that?" He knew exactly what it was. I simply smiled and said to myself, "Thank you, Mr."

After that, Sid went to bed like a good boy. The following morning he again tried to have sex with me. When I refused, he was quick to start packing his bags and he left in the leased car.

I was left with no return ticket, cash or car. He didn't say goodbye to Greg or Ron. He stormed out of the condo. Greg took control of the situation calling Sid and telling him he just couldn't leave me without my return airline ticket or transportation, and nowhere to stay for the remaining two nights, because their time at the condo ended the following day. On top of that Sid and I had made prior plans to travel across state and visit his brother who lived in Florida, a short distance away from Leesburg. Greg must have shamed him because he returned.

It was very uncomfortable between us and I couldn't imagine the next two nights with him. I told him we both needed to make the most of the next couple of days.

We got a hotel, and the next morning Sid went to his brother's house, and I walked to a nearby restaurant to get something to eat.

When he returned, he asked me if I would go with him to visit his brother later that day, and of course, I said yes. I knew his brother and sister-in-law were well aware that things were not going well between us, but I decided to make the best of the situation.

Once back in the room, Sid would watch sports and I would go to the pool or the computer room so we both stayed out of each other's way. When I came back to the room, Sid was watching sports on the television.

There was a terrible shooting pain in my jaw and ear, and I could not move my neck without pain. Sid said it sounded like an ear infection. I said it couldn't be. I never had an ear infection in my life.

I refused to go to the hospital, but after a few hours I could no longer take the pain. Sid took me to the emergency room in Leesburg. Another damn hospital visit, I thought to myself. This would be my fourth trip to the hospital in the fourteen months I had known Sid.

Prior to this round of hospital visits, I had not been to a hospital since I gave birth in 1967, and prior to that in 1958 with a kidney infection. Sid had caused me so much stress and I was so run down that my health was again suffering. It turned out that I had an ear infection and my blood pressure again was elevated at 190. I was given antibiotics and eardrops. The doctor said it was quite an infection.

We weren't in the hotel room ten minutes and Sid was trying to have sex with me again.

110

I was near tears. "Are you serious," I looked at him in amazement, "Do you realize how much pain I am in?"

He defended his actions and said, "I just want to hold you." He nagged and nagged, pouting with his lower lip curled, so I crawled into his bed and he went right for my crotch.

I started to feel as if I was being raped and I felt sick to my stomach. The roar and vibration filled the room again and as it did, Sid seemed to be swept right off the bed, as if a giant broom literally whisked him off the bed and onto the floor.

He stood there, bewildered and full of fear. The love and protection I felt from Mr. at that moment was deeper than anything I had ever experienced. Sid knew Mr. meant business and he left me alone after that event, and he became quite the "ass kisser."

Thank you, Mr.. I made it home and once inside my door I felt the safety and comfort of my small apartment. Sid said he was too tired to make the ninety-minute drive to his home and he asked if he could spend the night.

I said yes on the couch, and I gave him instructions not to wake me in the morning. I closed my bedroom door and smiled to myself as I crawled into my bed.

In the morning, I heard Sid leave and we both knew once that door closed he would not get back in. Oh, the emails and the calls came from him professing his love and apologizing over and over again.

Now that he was away from Greg's influence and I was on my own turf he was truly sorry. Sorry he had lost me – not for what he had done. He said he couldn't understand why he said the things he did. I asked him over and over again because I had to have an explanation why he said he did not know who Drax was or knew nothing about the tracks in the snow or the wet car and the orb we watched.

I pleaded, "Why, why, why? I just don't understand! Why?" He finally answered me, "BECAUSE I WANTED TO HURT YOU!"

On March 29th, during our vacation in Orlando, I received an email from a MUFON investigator that I had met at a MUFON meeting, one of the investigators with whom I decided to share my experiences. I was hoping he wanted to investigate. He sent me a letter of introduction and asked for information regarding my regressions and wanted to know with whom I might have shared my experiences.

111

He also wanted all of the messages I received from the aliens. He was extremely interested and I was excited because I thought I'd finally get to share with others. I told him I wanted to speak, and that would be the only way I would be able to heal.

He asked what I would be willing to share, and I replied, "Everything!" I don't think anyone can understand how important it is for experiencers to share their stories with others unless they are one themselves.

For fifty years I had held this inside of me and I was a volcano ready to erupt. When he told me I would be able to speak with the group of MUFON investigators I was elated. Finally... I would have a voice... Or so I thought.

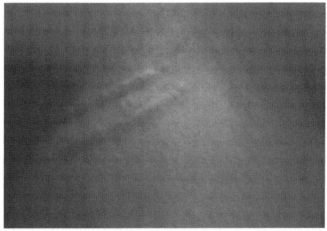

Drax Scratches

Breastfeeding and Bonding with Drax

Chapter 9
Doubt

An Excerpt from "Validation and Empowerment," by Steven Stosny, Ph.D.:

"Although necessary for growth, emotional validation is not growth. By definition emotional growth is transcending the limitations of our painful experience, which is much easier to do once it is validated, period.

In other words, emotional validation is not an end, but a precursor to healing and growth. An enriched life comes from the ability to see many perspectives in addition to our own experience. We all need compassion, to be sure, but just enough to be able to give it; personal power comes from giving compassion, not getting it."

There was no way that doubts about my relationship with the Reptilians wouldn't creep in with all of the negativity being hurled at me. I have been defending the Reptilians for so long, and the battle at times seemed almost futile.

My doubts about my relationship with the Reptilians and Mr. were certainly being put to the test. I had to at least entertain this information and question if any of it could possibly be true.

I would ask myself if they were so evil then why would their messages be so pure and beautiful? Why would they have allowed me to have my memories back? Why would they gift me with videos and illustrations?

The same answer would be thrown at me: "Because you are brainwashed!" If being brainwashed means to feel unconditional love and to be given a life with a purpose, then this is what I chose. Why would I be going through a healing process for the past four years if I were brainwashed?

Then, I happened to find this article: "How Belief Systems Affect ET Experiences," by Gwen Farrell.

This theory reduces all abduction experiences into two types: (1) The roller coaster ride you cannot wait to get back on, and (2) The roller coaster ride that makes you sick. Individuals in the first group felt unconditional love, they felt blessed, guided and protected. If given the choice, they would probably choose not to return to this life (or this Earth) next time they were taken.

We are the lucky ones (my opinion). The second group uses words like torture, rape and helplessness. These are the people who usually wind up in a therapist's office trying to find ways to forget. The research question comes down to "what if the positive or negative assessment of an ET experience is determined not by the actions of the ETs, but by the perception (or bias) of the experiencer?

Once we accept what is happening, we realize it is not about what the ETs are doing or not doing. It is about us, not them. As long as you accept and take your power you can get on with your life and face past and future abduction experiences as well as contact events without fear or anger.

I am again reminded of their message to me: "Perception is the way we perceive our reality." If we perceive our reality as positive, then we shall find that is how it really is. Had I listened to people's negativity my mission would have been lost. I realize now the meaning of one of their messages from early on in my journey to "enjoy the ride." I am. I truly am. Sometimes I need a break from the ride, but I always jump back on.

On May 18, 2013, I attended an experiencers group meeting and was delighted that I was able to share my videos and illustrations with the group. As I was driving home, I kept telling God, "Thank you, thank you!" I felt wonderful.

I sent this brief email to the group, "Hey, gang! I wanted to say thank you for helping me to heal. I wanted to thank you for believing in me." On May 20th, I received this email from one of the group members:

May 20th, 2015

Nancy, Always good to see you at our meetings. I don't usually have problems with words but your experiences left me humbled and a little afraid. When I finally saw all of your drawings in sequence with your explanations I was amazed at your bravery and I hope you can continue to keep speaking out and feeling more and more free to do so, and that you can own your experiences and put them in a normal context of life. I have never read or heard an abductee say "I am done here, I just want them to come and take me away..." That is a strong and powerful thing to say. Then, I listened to Landi who has had many intrusions in her life and declared that she has stopped being a victim and had been able to stop some abductions by saying "No!" and then one of them told her as she respected herself, so shall they. (It is) not too far from the golden rule "Love thy neighbor as thyself." So they, the Grays and Reptilians operate on fear and if we give in to our fear they will further victimize us. It was quite a day of learning. Thank you for telling your story."

Of course, I went into defense mode again, forever defending the Reptilians. I don't ever want them to stop taking me. My loyalty is to them. I have told them all "they" have to do is to keep directing me.

Anxiety and fear come from this Earth. I believe that my soul or "past self" has never experienced such negative emotions, and I believe they are attached to this planet. My friend Landi, the first person I met of "like kind" and "like mind" sent me an email after the group meeting telling me how far I had come since she first met me and how pleased she was that I was healing.

She said, "I know you are on your way to accepting who you truly are. It does us good to be in the same place as others who understand and let us know that there are others out there going through the same experiences. I still like Drax's little snow shoes!"

Nearly two months had passed and the email exchanges with the MUFON Investigator and I continued. I was still anxiously awaiting the promise he had made to me regarding speaking to other investigators.

It never happened. In fact, I wrote him again asking him to please call me as I was having trouble providing all of my information through emails. I gave him my number more than once and asked him to call. I did find it odd that he did not give me his number. I realized that he was just collecting information and I wondered what he planned on doing with it. Now, he was asking me for all of my regressions. This is something I have not been able to share. It is all I could do to listen to them myself. I wondered where this man got the nerve to ask me for something as personal as my regressions, and yet refused to talk with me over the phone.

On May 22, 2013, he sent this email in response to me asking him to call:

…Only email contact for now is a comfort level item. As our friendship develops I'm sure I will be comfortable with phone conversations. It is an unwritten rule voiced on many occasions with our state directors and trainers. A comfort level choice. What other events this summer in Michigan or nearby are you planning on attending? If none, I have a couple of trips planned where I will be going through Fowlerville on my way south looking for an opportunity where we can have more time to go over your events and transfer your regression recordings. Give me the details of your regression recordings, their length and purpose. Give me a short description of each. Once I know the recorded medium I can sort out a replication plan.

I knew at that moment he would never get another piece of information out of me. He was just collecting my information for his own personal purposes and never planned on giving me an opportunity to speak with other investigators. I sent Harry an email asking me if he thought it odd this investigator after nearly two months would not talk to me on the phone. Harry had been a MUFON state director in the past so I knew he would have the answers.

Harry told me he thought it was a bit unusual, and he was not sure about the comment "unwritten rule that is voiced on many occasions with our state directors and trainers. A comfort level choice?" He said he had never heard that one, but admitted he had been inactive for many moons and maybe there is somewhat of a new policy. He suggested running my concerns through Landi or someone I had come to trust.

Landi found the statement puzzling and said she had never heard of "comfort level choice." "Why would he choose not to talk to you on the phone," she asked. She said when she was working with investigators they came to her house. She said it seemed odd that he would be so reluctant to speak on the phone, and she had a hard time understanding his motivation. "It was my understanding that a field investigator went out to the site of the incident and spoke with all involved," making a point.

Dr. Willnus sent me an email instructing me to drop that particular investigator like a "bad habit," so in early July I sent him a message telling him that "…I no longer feel comfortable sharing with you and am now using different avenues." I blame myself for allowing it to go on for as long as it did. I have no hard feelings, as this was wakeup call for me. I am reminded of a quote I found on Facebook: "The people put in our paths are not always the ones we want but the ones we need to help us, to hurt us, to love us, to leave us." Now, I realize what he meant by "comfort level," a concept his wife made a rule.

I contacted a professor of sociology at Eastern Michigan University and a Ph.D. from the University of Chicago who took interest in my story and videos. He had been a consultant for NASA in the past and is involved with the Society for Scientific Exploration and author of several books.

He was going to try and set up a meeting with an expert in the interpretation of physical evidence and asked for my permission to forward my videos and pictures. Of course, once again this gave me great hope. He did call me that week and we spoke for over an hour. However, I didn't hear from him until four months later. He was apologetic, telling me he had been very busy.

I knew his wife had died; he was raising young children and working a demanding job. He told me David Jacobs, a professor at Temple University in Philadelphia, had told him that other abductees have been told to take the baton and run with it. I was starting to feel like that clown punching bag filled with sand we played with as kids. No matter how hard or how often you punched that clown, he bounced right back for more.

On June 22nd the state director was giving a library presentation in Fowlerville where I live, so I invited him, along with Harry and Roy my friend to my apartment for dinner prior to his presentation, which was only a block from my apartment.

I was very anxious to have him meet Roy and discuss the tracks and the missing time we had experienced together and for him to see where all of the "high strangeness" had been taking place. Harry, Roy and I were puzzled, to say the very least, when he spent an hour at my apartment and never asked one question of Roy or me. Not... one... single question. The day after the state director's presentation, Harry emailed him to inform him that we had contacted retired police chief Lee BeGole that night and that he revealed more about the 1961 incident, and that we had recorded the conversation.

I started to wonder if perhaps I was sharing with the wrong people. It sure felt that way.

Finally, a former MUFON field investigator confronted me with what I suspected all along. He wrote to me:

"Nancy, you apparently have an idea of what these UFO organizations are going to do for you and your needs aren't being met which is causing you great frustration. MUFON basically collects information, that's it!! They have also been infiltrated by the government. I guess if it were me I wouldn't be trying to convince anyone of anything just do what you feel is right for you. If you go public, there are going to be people who attack you. You have experienced some pretty scary shit! The public don't like to think such things are real. It is better to attack your character and call you a liar than accept that the Reptilian race is running around at night when we are supposed to be sleeping safely in our beds. MUFON is a volunteer organization not a funded professional organization. Most take on the guise of investigator in hopes of confirming what they are experiencing through others. The point is that this is a journey we must make on our own and you are starting that process. If MUFON cannot deliver, stop wasting your time and move on with information and friends you have picked up along the way, Yes, it is true that for some reason MUFON does not go out into the field and investigate. It was not that way when I was with the organization. I am afraid that this is just a shell of what the old organization was. Believe me when I tell you it was a much more dynamic organization then…"

Sometime after that the International director of MUFON at that time, David MacDonald, sent me an email telling me that I had some very compelling videos and that MUFON was very interested. By that time, however, I was done with it all.

"High Strangeness"

In June of 2013, I started experiencing what I call "energy voids." These periods would be brief, but for those few moments I would find myself in a vacuum of sorts void and empty. I seemed to be nowhere. I was told that this void is something experienced when one is traveling between dimensions.

On July 2, 2013, I woke up on my back, which is always my first clue I have been gone. I am a stomach sleeper and an avid pillow hugger.

Something was wrong. I felt as if I had just run a marathon. My left upper thigh felt as if there had been pressure put on it and my stomach area felt bruised and sore inside.

119

There was some sort of salve over my rectum and vagina, and I had a reddish rash between my inner thighs as well. I felt as if I had been vacuumed of all emotion and energy. I remembered the thin, silver metallic coiled tube they inserted into my anus. It reminded me of a vacuum tube. I thought to myself, "So, this is how they take your memories and emotions. They go right through your butt."

I also felt I had been vaginally examined. For the next four days I was totally exhausted. It was all I could do to make it from the bed to the couch where I would sleep on either one – wherever I fell. I even reached out to several members of the experiencers group seeking help.

I even managed a few tears over the course of those days, but it took too much energy to even cry. There really is nothing anyone can do for you when these events occur. You just have to ride them out. I was so depleted; I could not lift my arms above my waist! I had no appetite, either.

It was a very lonely and empty time spent trying desperately to recharge. It was odd that Roy was experiencing many of the same emotions! He told me he had never felt like that before. I feared I let him look into Pandora's Box.

Because I was so vulnerable and needed comfort, Sid was allowed to once again enter my life. It had been five months, and now he was back again. Apparently the Reptilians were not done with him either. Even though he returned, our relationship would never be the same as it was. I never allowed him to even kiss me again. He destroyed everything we once had, except for the sexual gratification.

On Saturday night, July 13, 2013, Sid and I were lying in bed. I was facing my bedroom window, and he was facing me.

In an instant an orange glow appeared and filled the entire bedroom. I could see nothing but brilliant orange. The orange glow seemed to leave the bedroom through the window with a brilliant flash of light. I screamed "*WHAT the FUCK!*"

We both jumped to our feet and made our way to the bedroom window to watch what was now an orange orb traveling at incredible speed, appearing to shrink in size as it sped away. We headed to the living room and went outside through the sliding glass doors onto my patio. I swiped up my phone off the coffee table as we did.

Once outside, we stood there in awe watching this orange orb "haul ass" until it was out of sight. We watched it for about another minute, and all the while I was fumbling with the camera on my phone trying to get the app started.

I finally did, but by that time, the orb was so distant, it would have been useless to try and get a decent video. On what we did record, you can hear me shouting at Sid, "Told ya... Told ya, you saw it! You saw it too! I told ya, see? See?..." Sid called MUFON and made a sighting report. One of my neighbors told me that her bedroom had lit up orange as well, even though she had the blinds shut. I believe that I was, or *we* were being returned from an abduction. I found it especially odd that Sid refused to talk about this incident and even got upset with me if I tried to talk about it. The following day I called Harry and placed the call on speaker because Harry wanted to ask Sid a question or two about the sighting. When Harry put forth a Question to Sid, he threw his hand up in the "stop" position and left the room. I apologized to Harry. I was so embarrassed.

Sid had a way of embarrassing me with his attitude toward other people. He was very jealous about my relationship with Harry as well. Sid would be rude to waiters and waitresses, and once ran up on a woman directing the parking at an event we were attending.

You could just imagine the bewilderment turning to fear as this 6 foot 6 inch man exited his car and ran to her, hovering over her flailing his arms and swearing.

He would always appear to feel terrible afterward, and apologize to me over and over again. Each time I would remind myself I did not even like this person. I never professed my love for Sid, because I didn't feel love. Much of his time with me was spent pouting and mad at the world. A couple of weeks after the orange orb, Sid and I had an argument, and he said, "I wish I never made that fucking MUFON report." "Why would you say such a thing," I asked. His answer still makes me shake my head in disbelief.

He replied, "Because we don't know who was flying that thing!" He then went on to rant and rave that he was never going to talk about it with anyone.

I told him he had to find out where all this anger was coming from, and why he chose to direct it toward me. I reminded him that this was not the first UFO we had seen together. It was the second. I said to him, "Don't you find that a little odd?" It was apparent the anger management classes he was taking were doing him no good.

In July of 2013, my youngest grandchild who was ten years old came to spend a couple of nights with me. She loves staying with "Baby Grandma" because she gets every second of my attention and I always go out of my way to have fun things for us to do.

She loves to draw and make crafts. We were sitting on the couch, and an invisible meowing cat decided to stand right in front of our feet greeting us both. Of course, there was nothing there; I do not own a cat.

Silence ensued, and after several seconds, my granddaughter said, "Grandma, you heard it, right?" I reassured her that I did indeed hear the cat. A few more seconds passed, and with an inquisitive voice she asked, "Grandma, where is it? Where is that cat?" "I don't know," I answered her.

We sat in silence for a long time as I tried to figure out what to say so I would not frighten her any further.

Finally, she said, "Yesterday when I was doing crafts I heard that cat." I could tell this was bothering her. "Oh, honey, why didn't you tell me?"

What she said next broke my heart, "Because I thought I was crazy." What a demonstration! Even at ten years of age she was afraid to mention the truth – something out of the normal range of experience – for fear of being thought crazy. The only reply I could make that might be considered consoling was "Well, you know weird things happen at Grandma's house…"

This phantom cat made a visit a few weeks earlier when a former MUFON investigator came to visit me.

He actually saw it as well as heard it. I was coming out of the bathroom when he asked me how long I had the cat. "I don't have a cat," I answered. I just saw it go into your bedroom, he replied. He asked if I heard it meow. I said I did. The investigator then went on to give me a description of the cat.

On August 1, 2013, Sid called me to tell me of an incident at his house the night before. His was a voice expressing the most emotion I had heard from him involving the odd events surrounding us. He sent me a picture of a red line on his bedroom wall, which he described as shiny bright red and looking like it had been made by a lipstick tube. He told me he ran his finger over it expecting it to smear, but nothing happened.

He said it measured about one inch wide and about three inches long and the temperature differed from the wall surrounding it. I still have the picture he sent me.

He said he got back in bed and continued to check on it until it finally faded away about three hours later. A couple of days passed, and I received a message from Mr. who told me to tell Sid "The writing was on the wall."

Needless to say, Sid did not find that comment funny in the least. (Author) Linda Poindexter said, "May you someday see the light, and when you do, may it not be so bright that you cannot see the writing on the wall." You cannot get any closer to the meaning Mr. was attempting to convey.

On August 6, 2013, Sid and I experienced missing time. We were watching "America's Got Talent," a television show we both enjoyed. They were going to commercial, and said when the show returned they would be announcing the winner. Realizing there was twenty-two minutes left in the show, I wondered how they were going to fill all of this time. I looked at Sid and said, "They're gonna milk this thing for twenty-two minutes."

As I finished that sentence we both looked at the television to see they had announced the winner. I checked the time again, and was 10:01pm. 23 minutes had passed in an instant. It jumped from 9:38pm to 10:01pm in a snap. I asked Sid what had happened.

"I don't know," he said, with bewilderment in his voice, "I have sitting right here with you!" I asked Sid "What was the last thing you remember?" He repeated my comment of "milking this for twenty-two minutes." I had to laugh because as much as Sid did not want to be a part of all this "high strangeness," he was! So, where were we for twenty-two minutes? In less than a month, Sid experienced the orange orb and missing time. The writing was on the wall.

On September 21st, 2013 I sent a group email regarding the next experiences meeting and informed everyone I would not be able to attend the next group.

Dr. Willnus and I agreed I needed some time to digest all of the "high strangeness" of the past few months. I simply was not ready to share and needed to step back. There was far too much going on in too short of a time period. I was running on emotional overload.

I broke it off with Sid, and this time it would last five months. He sent me an email telling me he was not the monster I thought he was. I wondered why he chose to use the word "monster" to describe himself, because I never used it in regard to him. His emails were full of apologies and undying love. His words held no meaning; at this time, I was numb.

On October 17th, Harry Willnus was giving a library presentation on UFOs, and he had promised to give me a few minutes near the end of his presentation to talk about my experiences.

It was a great turnout of about fifty people. I was on the edge of my seat, ready and waiting to speak. Before Harry introduced me, he asked the audience members if anyone knew retired police Chief Lee BeGole, and a young man immediately stood up announcing he had done an interview with BeGole a few years earlier about his World War II experiences.

I smiled and asked him if he would be willing to talk to me after the presentation. I spoke briefly of my Novi, Michigan sighting, and I was amazed that the audience was filled with so many questions.

Several people came up to shake my hand and thank me. The two female librarians told me how much they enjoyed my talk and wanted to hear more.

As Roy and I helped pack up Harry's car, Nick, the young man in the audience approached us and asked where we were going, and if he could join us. Of course we were anxious for any information he had regarding the retired chief BeGole. Nick had a lot of questions for me regarding my experiences, and he was fascinated with my illustrations. He asked for my number and said he would try to set up an interview with the former chief of police. Little did I know I would find this message on my answering machine:

October 25, 2013

Nancy, this is Lonnie Huhman, and I'm a reporter with the Novi News. I got an email from Nick Marroni telling me about a UFO sighting over Meadowbrook Road back in 1961. He mentioned your name and gave me your phone number, and I'm interested in doing a story about this. If you could, please give me a call back whenever it is convenient. I was hoping to get a story in the paper for next Thursday. I hope to hear from you. Thanks.

I called Lonnie within seconds of receiving his message, and we set up the interview for the following Monday, just three days later. I called Harry and asked him if he would be interested in joining me for the interview. It would take place in the exact spot I had that first experience in the summer of 1961. Of course, I had been to that spot several times over the years, but this time would prove to be different – much different.

I called Cindy, my childhood girlfriend who was also present for the 1961 UFO sighting. I told her about the interview but I didn't want to invite her though, out of fear she might show up intoxicated. It was important however that she verify that the event happened in the summer of 1961. I told her it was very important we were both absolutely sure of the year. I had been drawing an illustration of that day every year for fifty years and at the top of each picture I would write "The Summer of 1961."

Because Cindy was not 100% positive, I had to add the year 1962 as a possibility. Despite my frustration that Cindy could not remember the year, my validation would come in a couple of weeks from a woman that remembered that day very well, and indeed, it was 1961.

I barely slept the night before the interview. It was October 28th, and I was so very excited. I was the first one to arrive followed by Harry. The camera man and the reporter arrived and we all parked right in front of the area between my childhood home and Cindy's home. That interview allowed me to share my story and gave me the opportunity to reach out in hopes of finding others who were there that day and might be able to recall the event. I no longer had to keep my secret and worry about what others might think of me. After all, the chief of police at the time, Lee BeGole recalled it fifty years later. I was not crazy, and I was not making it up. It happened! It really happened, and no one could deny it.

After the interview, I had Harry pull up into the driveway of my childhood home. As we sat there staring at the house, memories flooded my mind and I knew what I had to do. I told him I was going to knock on the door of my house and get inside. I had no idea what magic words I might use to get me inside the house, but I was determined.

A woman of about forty years old answered the door. She looked as if she weighed 90 pounds, and she appeared to be about five feet tall. I did not want to scare her and I didn't know what words I might use, but I told her that this had once been my home and would she please allow me to come inside.

I told her I just finished an interview with a newspaper reporter regarding an event that had taken place many years ago and it would help me heal if I could just see my old bedroom. I pleaded with her to allow me in. She opened the door and I walked in.

I looked back at Harry sitting in the car and smiled and gave him a quick wave as if to say "I did it!" I took off my shoes and explained to her that I wanted nothing more than to look out of my bedroom window.

As I entered the bedroom, I couldn't believe how high the window was! No wonder I had to stand on my headboard! I started taking video with my phone, and it is obvious listening to my breathing that I was distressed. I stood on my tiptoes looking out at the exact spot where the ship hovered. My heart raced with excitement, and for those few moments, I was that little girl again standing on my headboard, looking out to the sky repeating those words I uttered with hopes, "Please come back and get me, please come back…"

Chapter 10
"Laveet..."

It is five o'clock in the morning on October 30, 2013. I awaken to find a small Grey Alien in my bedroom. He is so close to my right ear that I can feel the smoothness of his face brushing against my cheek. It feels like peach skin. I still cannot figure out why I did not feel any fear or surprise.

"*Laveet...*" He says to me telepathically. I had never heard that word before and I thought to myself that it sounded French.

I could not help but find humor in the fact that here, in my bedroom, standing so close I could feel him, was a French-speaking Alien. "Please leave me alone; I am tired," I thought to myself.

Now, for a second time this little Grey said, "Laveet!' a little louder. I knew exactly what he wanted. He wanted me to get out of bed and go to the computer and Google "Laveet" in order to find out the meaning of this word.

I tried to bargain with him telling him I would do it later, and to just let me sleep. "Laveet!!" he responded loud and clear, like he was implying "GET UP!" I get up, and with an inflating grudge make my way to the living room to turn on my computer, and as I start to Google, I realize I do not know how to spell the word. "Hey, wait a minute. How do I spell the word," I asked him with a bit of a sour look on my face. One by one the letters LA V E E T were placed clearly in my head. Inserting the word into Google, the definition clearly popped up. I was *not* thrilled! What was this guy trying to tell me?

"Laveet: Urban definition: Usually a female with curly hair and a curvy body... Very intelligent but stubborn... Extremely loud and crazy... Can be air-headed and perverse... Lively and fun to be around... Easily bored, mind-changing, competitive and determined... Jealous natured, but independent and strong... Laveets are unwilling to follow rules and are one of the most argumentative people you will ever meet. They will do what it takes to prove you wrong. No one can win with a Laveet, so be careful." (www.urbandictionary.com)

Well, needless to say that really pissed me off. I wondered why this Grey Alien had decided to make a 5am visit and force me to get out of my warm, comfortable bed in order to read about what a crappy person I was.

I headed back to bed confused and trying to make sense of this intrusion. At about ten o'clock I woke up at about my usual time, and my first thought was of the Grey Alien and the message he delivered earlier. I was curious and anxious to read that definition of Laveet again to see if it pissed me off as much this time.

It wasn't all that bad; I mean there were some redeeming qualities like "intelligent and stubborn," but "loud and perverse," or "argumentative?" I don't even like to debate, let alone argue. Am I really unwilling to follow rules? Was he really trying to describe me?

A short time later that day, I found out my interview with the Novi News reporter had hit the Internet. I tried to make the connection (if there was one) between why the Grey Alien would pick the same day my article is released to visit me and deliver that word.

"Laveet is not even a real word. You can only find it in the Urban Dictionary. I can only conclude that he was acknowledging my tenacity to be heard and possibly preparing me to be more of a Laveet.

Whatever the case, the word "Laveet" has become part of my vocabulary. Really, if I had not "Laveeted (my word…),'' I would never have been heard! I prayed that my story might reach people that remembered that day in 1961 to come forward. I sent the link to the interview to Vaughn and a few friends in the experiencers group.

On November 5, 2013, I received an email from Vaughn. It was the first email I received from him in several months. "Nancy, that was awesome," he said. He also congratulated me for being so courageous, and apologized for his absence, stating he had some things to straighten out.

On November 15th, I listened to an episode of "Spacing Out," on Open Minds TV. The hosts, Jason McClellan and Maureen Elsberry spoke of my experiences! Lonnie Huhman, the Novi news reporter forwarded me a few emails from people living in Michigan that had also experienced UFO sightings and wanted to share their stories. There was one very special email from a woman who remembered that day in 1961.

November 16, 2013

I read your article regarding Nancy Tremaine's experiences. I would be glad to talk with her as I had an experience (not quite as involved as hers), however.

128

It was in the summer of 1961, and in the next town over. I wish to remain anonymous about the incident and do not want to be published, but request that I share with Nancy Tremaine only.

Thank you for honoring my request...

There it was! It happened in 1961! I immediately sent her an email giving her my phone number and she called the very next day.

Our conversation lasted for at least thirty minutes and her voice never got above a whisper. I had to put the call on speakerphone so I could hear her more clearly.

It was obvious this event left a tremendous effect on her. She told me she was fifteen when this event took place in the summer of 1961. She was walking home from babysitting. It was about ten o'clock in the evening and the craft hovered above her and followed her as she made her way home. The craft was located just beyond the trees, and she could see it clearly.

A beam of light came out and began scanning the ground beneath the ship. She told me my illustration of the ship with the beam of light had validated her experience, and she thanked God when she saw the picture. She remembered the ship as being triangular in shape.

She made the run home, and once safe inside her house she told her father what she had seen. He went outside and of course, the ship was gone. When she told her other family members, they just laughed at her and no one believed her.

So she, like me, never mentioned it to anyone for fifty years, not even to her husband. It simply was not mentioned until this email to me. She told me she did not want to be regressed and that she did not believe they had taken her and that she had lived a normal life.

I wondered if she really lived a normal life. Having to keep a secret from a man you have been married to for over thirty years does not sound typical. Living a life with the fear of being ridiculed and laughed at also seemed to be far from being "normal," whatever normal means.

She only asked me one question in her whispering voice, "What do you think they want?" I thought that an odd question and it was clear from the sound of her voice she was still frightened, so I asked her if she *really* wanted to know, and she answered yes.

I told her the aliens were geneticists, and they were creating hybrids. The conversation ended quickly after that and I feared I would never be able to speak with that woman again, and I have not heard from her since that initial call. I sent her another email recently asking her to please contact me. I had more questions for her. Unfortunately, there has been no response. I pray she finds the peace she is seeking.

No matter how much evidence is produced, some people will never believe. Condemnation without investigation is the height of ignorance. Dr. John Mack has reasoned that to challenge or contradict an experiencer with a sacred quality is unethical. These people are bringing a truth from a higher dimension.

Calling Police Chief Lee BeGole

It was finally time for me to reach out to Chief Lee BeGole. One out of every four or five calls he will answer and this was one such phone call! His voice is strong and clear, and I detect he is anxious to talk.

I asked him if he remembered who I was and, with great conviction, he said he did. I knew he was aware of whom I was, but I found myself testing him – I had to know just what I meant to this man.

"Who am I?" I asked playfully and with a giggle.

He answered with no delay, "You're the lady who was very interested in the apparition over the skies of Novi. He added, "I distinctly remember that particular night. I haven't been able to locate anything in writing however, I know reports were made. In fact, it was mentioned in the Novi News."

"You think it was?" I asked him, telling him of my many trips to the library. "Oh, I know it was," he said firmly. Then I reminded him that he told me he might just have his own set of records from back then because he never threw anything out.

"I haven't located that," he replied, "I have a big job. I have a large frame home, and I never throw anything out. The place is just full of stuff." Then, after a short pause he added, "You know, I won't be around another twenty years, but I am too lazy and I don't do it!"

BeGole never married, so I can only imagine those papers are probably buried somewhere in his house. After he passes his family will just throw them away, and the answers I need so desperately will be gone forever. I explained to him just how important those records were. I explained to him how I live that night in 1961 over and over every day. I continue to try and refresh his memory:

"Don Young's wife was the one that called from their subdivision which is just off Novi Road, and I forget what the name of that subdivision was." I asked him, "What did she say when she called?"

"Oh, I can't remember the details, but I know that because of who her husband was and because he was a good friend of all of ours we paid particular attention to her phone call. Her husband Don was a city councilman. She saw this thing in the sky and wanted to report it. I also got a call from one of our own officers," the chief confirmed.

I questioned him further, trying to stir his memory, "What did she say when she called?"

The Chief responded to the question without pause, "Now, I can't recall at this time. I'm not making excuses but I have been extremely sick and it's going to take me some time to get back to normal." I explained to him how afraid I am that if something were to happen to him I would be lost.

"Well, you have just refreshed my ability to recall all of this, but not as well as my former abilities. I think there was something up there; I definitely believe it. We had an unmarked patrol car in the subdivision that was under construction. I think it was about nine mile and, uh, uh,"

"Meadowbrook," I interjected.

"Yes it was," he recounted, "There was a loss (theft), so we kept a car there every night, and we were reimbursed for it."

"Do you remember the year," I tested again.

"No, I can't recall the year," he replied.

I told him it was 1961, and late in the summer.

The chief replied, "Oh, yes it probably was way back then in '61."

I added, "You told me the car that was immobilized by the beam of light was one of your patrol cars."

"Possibly," he replied, "I'll have to think about it. It could have been."

He started coughing repeatedly, and I realized this conversation was about over. I explained to him that I wanted to talk with him again and that I feared I would not be able to reach him. I explained further that I was terrified because I didn't want to lose him, and that he was very important to me.

He reassured me, "You won't lose me."

"When can I call you again?" I asked.

He instructed me, "Anytime you wish except for Sunday mornings – I am usually in church. We'll have to meet. I can't just talk into a phone. Somebody's got to write down what I'm saying."

I was a bit apprehensive, and I felt guilty for not telling him I was recording our calls, but my life and my sanity depended on it. I told him I would call him once a week to say hello, and ask if you remember anything. I reminded him that if he remembered anything he should write it down.

He reassured me he would, "I absolutely will. The first thing I'm going to do, or try to do, is ask the librarian to locate something. What month was it in 1961?" I told him I believed it was August or September. I added it might have been in June or July, because the weather was nice, and it was summer.

"You were twelve years old I hear," he said. I did not mention this bit of information in our conversation. I felt we were moving forward.

"Yes," I responded, "My girlfriend was with me and her dad, and two policemen, and I think another neighbor and his children. There were several of us."

"I think you are clearing things up in my mind," the chief said. He sounded in better spirits than he did earlier. "I know it was in the paper. I definitely know it was in the paper. We had a very good local newspaper in those days."

"You know what would be better than the newspaper article," I added, "would be for you to find that original report."

"That's the objective," said the chief, "That's why I'm asking for the dates and the summer months."

I told him it was somewhere between six and eight o'clock in the evening and I was not allowed out after dusk.

The chief asked, "You were out, though, around dusk, right?"

I said I was. I continued, "My girlfriend Cindy remembered this event. It went from being light outside to being dusk, and when I was returned home it was dark! I was missing! I was gone! No one could find me! Do you understand what I am telling you?" I was getting bullish, trying to attest to just how emotional it all was for me.

"Yes, I do understand!" The chief replied, acknowledging this fact, "Did you live close to Nine Mile and Meadowbrook?"

That was it! He did remember! I supplied him with another clue. "I lived right on Meadowbrook. I was the seventh house on the left."

"Oh boy," he said. I knew at that moment memories were coming to him. I recognized the tone in the "Oh boy," and there was no doubt in my mind that he remembered. I added that he knew my dad, and he knew my family. "We were the Schingeck family!"

"Yes, things are starting to come back to me now," the chief said, "Thanks so much for talking with me and please give me a call in a week or so and maybe I will have turned something up. I would appreciate it so much. Now, for my own satisfaction too I am getting quite interested." I told him I would love to let him know what else happened. Then he might understand why this has haunted me my entire life. I added that I was messed up for a time, and I was starting to heal because I was remembering everything. I also told him that I had undergone hypnotic regression to assist in my recall.

"Well, this whole thing made a vivid impression on me and I can still recall it, and that's over forty years ago – maybe fifty. Thank you for calling and please call me again so we can compare notes to see what progress we are making." The chief really demonstrated great interest in my story!

I couldn't help it, I squealed "Thank you!"

He finished the call, "Well, thank you, and goodnight."

The February and March edition of Open Minds Magazine did an article focusing on my experiences.

I realize today the following messages "they" gave me two and three years ago were attached to the vision I'm about to be shown. The messages are as follows:

1.   "We are here to avert war. We are here to save you from yourselves."

2.   "You must learn to rule by love, not fear"

    And the most disturbing one,

3.   "Our messages are not for everyone. Many will be left behind."

Here is the vision to which these messages are attached:

I find myself aboard the ship and it is time for me to view an event of devastation. School is in session and I fear what I will be shown. I stand looking at the large windows that wind around the ship and as I look down I see a tremendous wind, and I watch the trees below the ship bend head first to the ground. Then the electrical poles begin to tumble, one by one by one. It is almost like I am watching slides in a viewer.

"They" quickly take me to the next scene and I see a large body of water filled with people struggling to stay afloat. Some wave their arms over their heads signaling for help. They remind me of bobbing apples. I am able to distinguish each individual's face and their unique fear. I am able to hear each individual's voice and their cry for help.

Suddenly the next scene begins and I watch as people on amusement rides fall to their deaths or are left hanging helplessly above the ground. I am overwhelmed with so many different scenes of death and destruction. "Why," I am wondering to myself, "am I watching this and I'm not a part of it?" I am told it is important I see these things and feel these emotions. I wonder if I am being shown the Earth to come or what it could be. I do not want to see anymore.

Pythagoras once said:

"For as long as man continues to be the ruthless destroyers of lower living beings, he will never know health or peace. For as long as men massacre animals they will kill each other. Indeed, he who sows the seeds of murder and pain cannot reap joy and love."

I look back and see that I had done a lot of reaching out in hopes of being heard. Most people never responded, however, I never gave up. I continued to be a "Laveet."

Ufologist Responds!

In February of 2014, one very well-known female ufologist and alien abduction researcher, author and hypnotist did get back to me to tell me she had little patience for "Stockholm syndrome."

She continued to tell me that although there may exist some neutral aliens out there that do not harm us, abduction for the most part is not a good thing. It is not good for our souls or our true freedom from their parasitism. She suggested if I wanted a more sympathetic pro-alien researcher or therapist, Barbara Lamb might be more suitable for your needs.

She encouraged me to look into the work of Dr. Corrado Malanga from Italy. It is her belief he has nailed it in terms of what the aliens are really after, and various corporeal and incorporeal beings working behind the scenes from a parasitic perspective and feed on human soul energy.

They live through us in order to maintain a kind of immortality. Most of them lack an eternal soul as we do. They must use our divine connection to God (or the Source) to maintain their existence. They want to do this however at our expense by repressing our true essence and spiritual growth.

She also addressed the heightened sexual energy and said it is tied to "life force prana" and that is a drug or an elixir to the aliens. They want us to produce this energy so they can use it for their own purposes.

One of the processes they use to amp up our sex drives and energy is through pheromone programming and manipulation of the chakra energy centers through implants. It is a type of parasitism that is quite effective at boosting our sexual energy. These beings can give us great sexual pleasure and they know how to activate this even to the point of addiction. They can also use this against us, for their own agenda, and ultimately, it hurts us.

It was amazing, she said, that I had a child at the age of 62 and that I was still so sexually active. She asked me if, during one of my many regressions, did I ever have former life memories of having made prior soul agreements with these beings and if I had done so, did I wish to change the nature of that agreement or cancel it altogether.

She suggested I might want to consider this. It is her opinion that aliens can manipulate our perception to their advantage, and they will do this through parasitism or a kind of "attached entity' phenomenon and through implants which affect our energy centers.

She said if we can connect authentically to the highest divine part of ourselves, our soul, then we can use this connection, awareness and power along with out will to remove the interference in order for us to detach from their manipulation. Then, and only then you will be able to discern the true nature of your experience – the truth about what is happening to you. She finished by saying she had probably lost me by now. She said if I was really hurting (and she was sure I was hurting), I might want to consider another view of these aliens who have "used you" all this time.

I responded to her:

"I want to thank you for taking the time to email me and provide me with information I have already begun to research. I have an open mind and try to see both sides of everything. Maybe you are right about the Stockholm syndrome. My life has not been easy. I have never been able to hold down a job or maintain a relationship with a man. I live in a small one-bedroom apartment. I spend several days in a row locked in and

away from everyone; I have always done that. It has only been since September of 2011 that I have allowed myself to remember the abduction of 1961. Things are going so fast. My life is filled with high strangeness and when one thing ends, something new starts. I hear your anger and distrust toward the aliens and I can feel your frustration with me. I know you see me as weak, allowing what you call parasites to attach themselves to me. I'm sorry if I make you feel these things. In response to your question about past lives, yes, I have always known about some of my past lives and even how I died. You are right when you suggested I might have volunteered for this mission. I fear your hatred if I told you I thought I might be more than a volunteer but a part of them. I have tried to write you all day, but kept deleting because I am so emotional and unsure of what I can say. My mother always hated my honesty. She told me that sometimes when someone asks you a question they don't really want an answer.

On February 25th, 2014 I received her response:

Thank you for sharing your honesty about my response to you and what you sense as anger and hatred. It certainly is not directed to you personally, but my own feelings about aliens and what they have done to me, close friends and others that have caused a lot of harm. I take responsibility for my own feelings and do not want to project them on you in a way where you don't feel comfortable with being honest. So, I apologize for this. It's complex, and we are finding that there are more connections than current life interactions with these beings and there might very well be a co-creative aspect to our experiences. What is important is to be able to have the opportunity to feel safe. Maybe what we hold are these entities' memories that are the aspect of them inserted into us so they can live through us. Again, I apologize if I came on too hateful to you. Warm regards...

I respect this woman and her beliefs and I thank her for taking the time to share with me. We must always remain open.

It is March 9, 2014. It is one day after Malaysia Flight 370 disappeared. My two friends Tom and Roy called me that day. Roy asked me what "my buddies" had done with the plane. Tom asked me where the plane was.

I told both of them the same thing: "I don't know what happened to the plane, but I do know they will never find it." I said that out loud every day for months and would scream at the news reporters as they continually ran coverage of the search. "The plane is gone!" Months and months went by and the search continued. Every day I would scream at the news and I kept saying "what a waste of money and time...the plane is gone!"

A friend and I had been working on a plan to get me to Arizona, as I am really not a Michigan person. I cannot tolerate the cold weather and even as a child disliked the snow and never enjoyed playing in it. The spring in Michigan is intolerable as I have such severe allergies that cause my eyes to actually swell shut.

Even my primary physician has told me to move away from Michigan. Alas, my finances, or lack thereof, kept me tied to the state. Sid promised me he was going to get me to Arizona.

He even flew out to Arizona for a job interview which he did not get, and he even made a second trip to look at apartments in Arizona while he was visiting his son in Texas. I must admit it was tempting to move, and there was a short period of time in which I would have sold my soul to get out of Michigan. We both knew in our hearts it was never going to happen.

On May 23, 2014, I reached out to a woman in England. She is an experiencer, speaker and artist. She told me that unlike America they do not have much in the way of self-help groups but was working with AMMACH (Anomalous Mind Management Abductee Contactee Helpline). One of her early abductions involved her and a girlfriend, and she too would not be able to remember her experiences for many years. We shared stories and found comfort in each other's words.

She worked as an electronics engineer for a firm called Marconi. Marconi made the headlines in the 1980s as being one of the major contributors in the "Star Wars" project, or the United States Strategic Defense Initiative.

When she arrived for work one morning in the late 1970's she noted the security guards were not in their places and instead noticed an MoD (Ministry of Defense) parked outside.

137

Throughout the morning she witnessed high-ranking military people huddled together. She was asked to pick up work from an outside contractor. Being nosy, she decided to take a different route into work and found newly placed "Strictly No Admittance" signs strategically placed and realized that no engineers were in sight. The story over the water cooler was that a security guard doing his late-night rounds saw a blue light emanating within the Top Secret area. He then entered the room where the light had come from and found a grey alien rifling through the Top Secret documents.

He was wearing headgear that shone with a blue light. When the alien noticed the security guard in the doorway, the alien waved his hand and disappeared into a cloud of light. The guard was taken away by military psychiatrists and never seen again.

A couple of months later, she overheard a conversation by the director telling whomever was on the other end of the phone "…if these beings can come and go with all the security we have, what the hell can we do? We are totally powerless to do anything. They can get in anywhere – any facility in the country!"

From 1982 to 1988 no less than twenty-five scientists from Marconi were found dead, and presumed to have committed suicide or had a fatal accident. Many of those cases are still open.

On June 14, 2014, Ken Parsons, the founder of BEAMS Investigation (The British Earth Aerial Mysteries Society) released a video he made of my experiences on Youtube entitled "Footprints in the Snow."

I was thrilled and filled with gratitude that he had acknowledged me. Shortly after that I received an email from the Novi, Michigan news reporter who interviewed me commending me on my efforts and encouraged me to "keep it up." *Long live Laveet!*

On June 18, 2014, I was awoken as my cat, "Cuddle Bugs," jumped in bed, landing on my legs. I lifted my head and waited patiently as she made circles around my right calf trying to find a comfortable position. I smiled with contentment as I laid my head back down on the pillow. Suddenly, I sat up in bed somewhat mystified. Cuddle Bugs had been dead since 2009!

On June 23, of 2014, I sent an email to an author and a former secretary to Dr. J. Allen Hynek. She is a researcher, speaker and author. She also worked in the White House during the Clinton administration. I gave her a link to my video and shared my recurring dream of being surrounded by the ships and orbs, accompanied by feelings of overwhelming love.

I told her about my son, Drax. I really never expected a response from her so I was elated when she got back to me so quickly! Here is her response to me:

June 23, 2014

Hi, Nancy!

Thank you for contacting me. Bless you and Drax. It is all real, and I think wonderful. Thank you for being brave enough to put that video out. We now have fifty percent of the world's population that have been contacted and receiving information from the ETs into their subconsciousness. Soon, all will know that it is real. As Earth changes increase we will be seeing the ETs more and more and when we are near, and during the pole shift they will openly be helping us. You have obviously instrumental in the creation of the new alien hybrids race. They will be inhabiting the Earth in about 100 years.... wonderful beings. The scene of all the ships in the sky is a universal vision. We all have seen it, and it will happen...

On June 24th I sent her an email thanking her for responding and how much I respected her work. I also told her I had started writing my book and that all I wanted to do was to share all of my information with the world, and was hoping to do it as a speaker. I then told her to feel free to ask me any question as there was nothing I would not answer. Our correspondence continued:

June 24, 2014

Hi, Nancy!

Write the book and that will be used as your calling card for speaking engagements. You will notice that all speakers have at least one book out. It will never make you rich, but it will be your entre' to the podium. How wonderful that Drax will be a "wise judge." We sadly need one. I have asked so many questions over the

years that I am all questioned out. Just waiting for the
real action to begin.

This woman has no idea how much her emails meant to me. She is a positive in a world filled with so much negative. Thank you my friend.

On June 24th, out of desperation, frustration, and several attempts to reach Chief BeGole I was determined that he was going to hear me out. He was not going to be able to change the subject or cut our conversation short like he had for nearly two years every time I got close to telling him what he already knew.

I left him this message: "Chief BeGole, this is Nancy Tremaine. I have tried to have this conversation with you for nearly two years and I fear your passing and my not being able to tell you. I think you know more than a UFO sighting happened that day in Novi.

I was taken. I didn't talk about this for fifty years. I have been in therapy, and through regressions I remember. I remember! My father and the police could not find me. I know! We need to talk about this. Please. I have so much to share with you. This has all been so traumatic. Please call me back."

After I left that message, I regretted doing it and worried I had possibly scared him off. On July 4th I called and left a short message on his answering machine telling him happy birthday. He was now ninety four and I knew time was running out!

Chapter 11
The End of the Road

<u>The Prayer</u>

I pray you'll be our eyes and watch us where we go
And help us to be wise in times when we don't know
Let this be our prayer when we lose our way
Lead us to the place
Guide us with your grace
To a place where we will be safe
I pray we'll find your light
And hold it to our hearts
When Stars go out each night
Let this be our prayer
When shadows fill our day
Lead us to a place
Guide us with your grace
Give us faith so we'll be safe
We ask that life be kind
And watch us from above
We hope each soul will find
Another soul to love
Let this be our prayer
Just like every child
Needs to find a place
Guide us with your grace
Give us faith so we'll be safe

"The Prayer" by David Foster
Sung by Andrea Bocelli and Celine Dion

Barely a day has gone by in the past three years that I haven't listened to this song and felt a connection to the Reptilians. Sid was in the bathroom when the phone rang but he could hear me screaming when police "Chief Lee BeGole" popped up on my phone's screen.

Instead of sharing in my excitement, he mumbled, "Well, there goes our evening." He knew me well, and he knew after that phone call I would be running through the apartment jumping up and down

141

with excitement. I scrambled to find my tape recorder and quickly catch every word.

On July 14th of 2014 Chief Lee BeGole and I would have our last conversation over the phone. He said, "You called, and Happy Birthday was on my answering machine."

I said, "Yes, you turned ninety-four!"

He thanked me for the call.

I said to him, "You're still just a kid!"

"Yeah, just a kid," he replied, with humor in his voice. After a moment of mutual silence, we both laugh and I tell him he sounds great, and he really does!

"Well, I feel pretty good," He began, "You know I had double Pneumonia. I went to the hospital and that was quite an ordeal, too. You know what? There was an article in the paper, the Novi News, way back about your spaceship. That was, uh... I'm trying to recall now, but right after I talked to you last I went into the hospital and I didn't get a chance to tell you about it, but there was definitely something in the paper. Somebody told me about it, and I can't recall who it was."

I inform him that I spent hours at the library going through the archives every month... he interrupts, "It was in there!"

I ask him if he can remember the names of the police officers.

"Martin Cone," he answered, "He went down to a Cherokee reservation. He did pass away. He lived on the border of Tennessee and North Carolina living on that reservation. He was half Cherokee."

I asked him if he could remember the other two officers.

"No," he replied with a bit of frustration in his voice, "I should but I... It's really been too many years. I went to the hospital in Detroit and had the diagnosis of tuberculosis and my niece, a nurse, came down there. I didn't have TB; I was given the wrong diagnosis!

I went in there for bronchitis and they couldn't figure out why I couldn't breathe. It turned out to be a rare and very powerful infection. I just put things off and I know I told you I was going to do this...

Kathy Mutch – have you talked to her? She used to be on the city council. She knows how to dig things out of the history of Novi. I'll give her your phone number but it will take a couple of days. Listen, I just called briefly to thank you for the birthday call and to let you know I hadn't forgotten you and I will be working on the case. Not tomorrow, but soon.

I will do all I can do... I know that (craft) was up there because I heard Martin on the radio and I talked to Mrs. Young, the councilman's wife and I remember that night because I went down there later on."

"What did you see," I asked, and I told him I heard there was a mark in the grass where it had been, and nothing grew there for quite a while.

"No, they didn't show me that," he stated, "But I went down and met Martin on the scene, and he pointed out where it was, and it was gone. It took me two to three hours to get down there. Officer Cone didn't come back to the station yet… pardon me, he did, but only for a minute because Mrs. Young called and he went back."

So, now I am being told that officer Martin Cone made two trips to the scene. The second trip was made right after he returned to the station. This confirms my regression memories of being returned and seeing no one was there at that point.

When "they" dropped me off I looked up at the ship and was told, "See, we told you we would get you back safely." So, this must have been when Mrs. Young saw the ship – it was when they were returning me.

This was very important information he was giving me and he was remembering it as we were on the phone. This also confirms what the aliens had promised regarding abductees and the supposed "Eisenhower Treaty (Abductees would be returned to where they were abducted, and unharmed)." I am very curious why it took him two to three hours to go to the scene as he was the police chief and the station was only a few minutes away.

"Well, don't you worry," said the chief, "There was a craft there and I think we will get the documents to prove it."

"I sure hope so," I said. I then reminded him how important it is to meet face to face with him.

He reassures me that we will meet at the restaurant by the railroad tracks near my apartment. Every time we spoke I knew in my heart that I would never be able to pin him down or get a time and a day to meet, and I realized I had probably gotten all of the answers he was capable of giving me.

I still continue to call however, and leave messages. He will be ninety-five years old in July of 2015. I was forever grateful for the information he did provide. Thank you, Police Chief BeGole.

In June and July of 2014 Sid and I continued to entertain the idea of moving to Arizona but we both knew it was only a pipe dream.

My sexual desire had all but disappeared, and we had not even kissed each other for almost a year. It was becoming apparent there was no romance left.

As I said earlier in the book, by August of 2014 Sid and I had broken up at least four times. This time, it felt completely different. I asked Sid to return all the items I had left at his house and we knew this was "the end of the road." We both sat on the couch looking at each other.

I placed my hand gently on his thigh and looking him in the eyes I said, "We both know this relationship is over."

He asked, "So, this is it?" Like a total idiot, I tell him we can still be friends. He asked me if he could hold me and I allowed him to wrap his arms around me for what I felt was the last time. He is a very predictable man. What did he do? He went right in for the crotch.

I pushed him away, and as I did, he groaned, "I thought we'd have sex one more time before the last time." "What the hell does that mean," I thought, "…one more time before the last time?"

I stood up immediately and headed for the kitchen to retrieve a plastic bag, then headed for the bathroom, tore back the shower curtain and grabbed his shampoo and body wash. His eyes followed my every move as he sat with a pouting look on his face.

He heard the medicine cabinet open and heard his toothbrush and assorted other things he left there being thrown in the bag as well.

Finally, he heard the closet door in the bedroom swing open as I grabbed his lounging pajamas and boxer shorts he left there. I returned to the living room and I had to fight back a smile because I couldn't get past his remark. I dropped the bag on the dining room table.

He stood up, grabbed the bag and without a word walked out my front door. I turned the lock and pressed my back against the door and took a deep breath. I realized it was the first deep breath I had taken since I met him. We have not said a single word to each other since that day eleven months ago, and as I am writing this book we have still not spoken.

It is the summer of 2014, and the time was shortly after my final breakup with Sid. I was walking in the park behind my apartment complex when I suddenly felt myself start to rise and actually detach from my physical body. It was the strangest sensation and I was acutely aware of what was taking place, and I allowed it, I even welcomed it!

As I rose above the terrain, I could actually see myself walking! I thought to myself how very small I was and suddenly realized I had become the girl in the picture I have in my living room living room – I became the girl in my illustration. The girl in the picture was walking on a lonely dirt road surrounded on both sides by tall pine trees.

I was suddenly aware of an incoming message, "You are almost at the end of the road; enjoy the ride." I smiled to myself and felt contentment, "How wonderful!"

On August 7th I sent an email to Vaughn. In it I explained the hardest part of this process had been to listen to the regression. I told him that I never really listened to them and that I now realized why the fifth regression was the final one for him.

I told him, "I understand now how you felt 'they' were manipulating me. I chose this mission, and would never take it back." I told him I had copies of regressions two, three and five, and let him know that the fourth regression of January of 2012 accidentally got deleted.

I told him I was sick about losing it. I told him "I don't even remember what was revealed in that regression. It took place five days after I met Sid and less than a month before I would up in the hospital.

Please Vaughn, tell me you have a copy, or at least remember what was revealed during that regression. It is so important to me, and crucial for my book." I told him I needed it for my own sense of personal wellbeing.

I told him,

> *Writing this book is the best thing I could be doing. I never wanted to write a book, but a researcher and author and my cousin Chris have strongly encouraged me to write this book. With each chapter I feel able to move forward and put what happened behind me. I know we haven't spoken in a long time Vaughn, and you would be shocked to know all that has happened and continues to happen in my life. I haven't shared with anyone because there is so much to share! I know fear sells books, but my experiences with the Reptilians are welcomed and not feared. The videos and the pictures I have are gifts from them. The witnesses are also gifts.*

The messages continue to come and my connection with them is pure love. Those marks on my chest after a visit with my Drax were a hologram. There was no physical pain or feeling to them. Those claw marks were a gift to let me know I had been with Drax and that we had bonded. It is odd how many experiencers use the words 'in hindsight.' I have lots of illustrations now. I think of you often and never want to lose you. Your friend always...

On August 11th I received Vaughn's response. His tone was optimistic. And his words were supportive. He said,

Nancy, I am thrilled to hear about your book. I don't have a transcript for the fourth regression, but I do have a good memory for all of the regressions, at least on the salient points and direction of the narrative. I will call and we can go over what each one of us might be missing. I have done approximately one hundred past life regressions over the years. Your experience is the only one that I have had the privilege to do in regards to alien abduction. I haven't any doubts as to your credibility. I'll call soon. May God bless all of your endeavors
-Vaughn Vowels

On August 20th, I returned Vaughn's email saying:

"I know you're busy but I would appreciate anything you could write me regarding my fourth regression, or anything you feel would be important during any of the other regressions. Chief BeGole called me to tell me he hadn't forgotten me, and he added a new detail. Sometime after police officer Martin Cone said "Strange object overhead..." he returned to the police station and was called back to the scene for a second time. So apparently, the ship returned. I believe this is when "they" dropped me off. BeGole is ninety-four and he sounds great. I did have to laugh to myself when he stated "I am on the case!" I have been to the Novi library and have gone through all of the archives and didn't find anything. BeGole and others I have been in touch with swear they remember an article but no one was able to produce it. I hope to hear from you soon.

Nancy

Vaughn came over to my apartment the following week. It was wonderful having Vaughn back in my life and I felt thrilled to be able to share all my new illustrations and messages with him.

Vaughn accepted my relationship with the Reptilians. It was not important that he agreed with them, but it was important he was able to understand the mission I was given. During our conversation we even discussed possibly regressing my girlfriend Cindy – if she were to consent.

On September 8th I sent another email to Vaughn:

...Cindy has definitely quit drinking. She had some kind of divine intervention while attending a "retreat," and it has been over three weeks since she had a drink. She is also beginning to experience what I went through at the beginning of my journey. She is filled with questions, and seems ready to talk about what she remembers, and she remembers a lot. She is very interested in having a regression. I think she needs this, and I also think it is important to her healing. Do you think we can set something up for the month of October at my apartment? I will record the regression. I am curious to see what she has held inside her for all these years.

Your friend, Nancy

Vaughn returned my email on the same day, "Nancy, any Friday in October would be great and I will bring a tape recorder. I hope Cindy continues her recovery..."

Remember Skinny Bob? I found myself obsessed with him because I had so many unanswered questions. Why did my father go on a business trip to California right after that first sighting in 1961? It was the only overnight business trip he ever took, and I mean ever! And most odd was the fact that he was offered a company position in Australia?

Thinking back, this was quite troubling. I chose to send an email to a man that is regarded as one of the leading authorities on the "top secret" Majestic 12 intelligence documents and the 1941 Cape Girardeau, Missouri UFO crash.

He was engaged in deciphering the physics of UFOs while managing a research project on anti-gravity for McDonnell-Douglas. I figured there was no one better qualified or knowledgeable on this subject than he.

On September 19th I wrote my first email to him:

... My father told me about Skinny Bob in 1961 after I was abducted in Novi, Michigan. Please Google my story. My father drove for General Ennis Whitehead during World War II. How would I have knowledge of something that wasn't made public until 2011? My father was a Hydraulics Engineer and worked for the government. What will it take for someone to listen to me? I am currently writing a book as I feel this is the only way I can get all of the information out into the open. I have been an abductee since I was two years old, I have been regressed five times, and the witnesses I have include a former police chief, an attorney, a fireman who is also a farmer, a former prison guard and a former MUFON field investigator just to name a few. I have a girlfriend who was witness to my abduction in 1961. My main question is, was General Ennis Whitehead one of the people at the 1941 UFO crash in Missouri? It is my belief that this is the crash when Skinny Bob was captured. When my father told me he was called Skinny Bob my first response was "how cruel that is!" We humans were bullies then and we are still bullies! Pretty sad a twelve-year old recognizes how sick that was.

Truly,

Nancy Tremaine

On the same day he replied to my email:

Thanks, Nancy for the comments. We don't know much about who was at the crash in 1941 other than Reverend Huffman's Testimony. I am all ears if you know someone who was there. As for Whitehead, he was a Lieutenant Colonel back in 1941. It's possible he was there, but a little junior, but had intelligence experiences. I'll try to call late next week.

On September 25th, he called and we talked for almost an hour. I told him all I could remember about my conversation with my father regarding Skinny Bob. He wanted a copy of my father's military records, and I said I'd gladly provide them. I sent him a letter with copies of letters my father had written during World War II that had mentioned his relationship with Pappy Gunn and General Ennis Whitehead. I believe it was one of these two people who told my father about Skinny Bob.

On the same day I received a copy of his book and a beautiful letter. I could not put it down and read the entire book in two days. He thanked me and told me he enjoyed our conversation and encouraged me to let him know of anything else I might come up with. He added that he looked forward to receiving my dad's military records.

On October 6th, 2014 I asked him in an email if he had ever heard of Pappy Gunn before I mentioned him earlier in one of our conversations. I also told him I wanted to find family members of General Whitehead. I told him that Skinny Bob had become an obsession, and I wanted to provide Skinny Bob a voice and give to him the respect he deserved.

He answered my email and sent me a link so I could order my dad's military records. He told me he had not heard of Pappy Gunn but said there was a lot of information on him. He asked if I would share any messages the Reptilians would send me regarding the future, and if any of their previous insights have come true.

It was October 9th, and I sent him an email expressing my beliefs in the Reptilians and their agenda and told him about my son, Drax. I shared several messages I received from the Reptilians. I also told him I sent for my father's military records. I told him I found it refreshing that aboard the ships men run the show and women nurture just like God intended, and lightheartedly said that this observation is not always received well by other women.

I informed him that I had sent for my father's military records four weeks earlier and would send him a copy as soon as I received them. I mentioned a long conversation I had with Nathaniel Gunn, the son of Pappy. Unfortunately, his father was not the person who told my dad about Skinny Bob. I tried to find relatives of General

Whitehead but have had no luck so far. Giving up however is not an option.

"Good attitude, Nancy!" he responded. I gave myself a pat on the back. He asked if there was a MUFON group meeting coming up. At least the people there have open minds.

On November 18th I emailed him and told him my experiences with MUFON have not been positive and I do not feel comfortable with them. I shared the information a former MUFON investigator here in Michigan had told me and how things are run very differently now.

There are no more boots on the ground here; and there is government infiltration. I told him my instincts tell me to distance myself from the organization. In closing, I told him how much I loved his book and that I was unable to put it down. I read it in two days.

In his return email he told me that he knew the current international director very well and that he could pass along my concerns to him easily and anonymously if I desired to choose that option. He added the investigation teams change constantly, and that Colorado has changed several times over the past ten years. I truly appreciated his offer regarding MUFON.

I explained that I would be in many of the same places as some of the members of Michigan MUFON in the future, and I did not want to feel any more uncomfortable than already did with this situation. In hindsight I wish I had never mentioned the word MUFON.

On December 16th of 2014 I contacted him through email to tell him I had received notice that a copy of my dad's military records would be sent out the second week of February 2015. They were backlogged five months!

I felt bad for even mentioning MUFON to him and explained that perhaps I expected more from them than they were able to provide. As experiencers we are all reaching out in the only way we know how and we are asking to be heard, believed, and respected. My problem was not with MUFON, but with a few people involved with the organization, I felt like they dropped the ball when it came to my case, and probably experiencers overall.

At my apartment I have shoeboxes filled with letters my father sent to my mother across the three years of his deployment, and seem to be continually drawn to one letter from him to my mother while he was at Tachikawa Air Field in Japan dated September 20th, 1945. It is my belief this is when my father learned of Skinny Bob.

At the time, my father was asked by his Commanding Officer to drive General Whitehead, a three-star General and Commander of the 5th Air Force, around the base and then into Tokyo to see how badly the city was ruined after we dropped the first atomic bomb ever used in wartime on the city. The General also wanted to find quarters for the occupation forces. That was a great deal of time to converse and get to know one another, and General Whitehead had a strong background in intelligence. General Whitehead respected my father and gave him the Company Commendations of Asiatic Pacific Ribbon with one bronze star and the Philippines Liberation Ribbon with one bronze star. He acknowledged my father had been in over one hundred air raids and well over a hundred days on the water traveling, driving trucks for the Air Corps, and hauling essential supplies.

This seemed to be quite an accomplishment for a man of only twenty-two years. It was also a time of the Foo Fighters. A term used by allied aircraft pilots in World War II to describe various UFOs or mysterious aerial phenomena seen in the skies over both the European and Pacific theaters of operation.

On September 28th I contacted Vaughn to let him know that Cindy's regression was still on for the 17th of October unless Cindy's husband's health got worse. Cindy's husband had been clinging to life for several months. I was also concerned that Cindy was drinking again. She denied it – but I know her all too well. I signed off telling him I would see him soon.

Another Vision

The following is by far the most difficult process they put me through. The Reptilians need to evoke and study the emotion of empathy. It was very difficult to write these words out on paper. Even in the present, they feel so real and so raw. The Reptilians tested me with another vision. The Reptilians show me a newborn piglet and it is *precious*. It is tiny and pink and they are feeding it from a bottle the size of a baby doll's bottle. Then, they show me a hot griddle and I fight them begging that they please not do this. They slowly place the baby piglet on its side on the hot griddle. The baby spits out the bottle's nipple and starts to cry. It sounds just like a human baby. I am beside myself with terror and want to rescue this little baby. The piglet struggles to rise up but can only manage to lift its head and shoulder until a long, clawed finger gently strokes the baby, pressing it bank down on the griddle. As the baby spits out the nipple for the

151

second time to cry it is caressed by this clawed finger and is pressed back down on the griddle and the nipple is once again pushed gently back into the baby's mouth. "Oh my God! Please stop!" I begged them. I could not watch this. It was the most helpless I have ever felt, and it was the most horrific torture I had ever seen.

They tried to explain that it was just a vision and nothing more, but I could not understand and I began to wail uncontrollably. I was furious with them and I told them I don't care that it is necessary for me to feel these emotions just so they can study them. I screamed, "Don't do this to me again!"

John E. Mack in his book "Abduction: Human Encounters with Aliens" states:

> *I am often asked how experiences which are so traumatic, and even appear cruel at times, can also be spiritually transformative. Sometimes our most useful spiritual learning and growth come at the hands of rough teachers who have little respect for our conceits, psychological defenses or established points of view. Zen Buddhist teaching is notorious for its shock treatment methods. One might even go further and argue that spiritual growth is inevitably disturbing, as the boundaries of consciousness are breached and we are open to new domains of existence. This, of course, does not 'forgive' the cruelties associated with alien abduction...*

There is nothing more important to an experiencer than to find someone that "gets it." It's so vital to find someone who tries to understand and empathize.

My cousin Chris is such a person. Even though he knew how difficult this journey of mine would be he continued to encourage me by telling me just how important it is for me to finish this book. Thank you, Cousin Chris. I want to share an email I received from Chris on September 8, 2014, when he said,

> *I have to remain open. I can't imagine the alienation you must feel having experienced what you have and been so unable to expect anyone who has not had these experiences to understand. Every time I close the door to the barn at night when the chickens go back in their coup I glance at the sky afraid, yet*

152

hoping I might catch a glimpse of an alien craft. I also think it is good you are away from Sid. It's too bad you had to add those experiences to your life, but if the intention is a learning experience I guess it is at least worthwhile, as long as you are allowed one day to meet someone of the opposite who you will be very attracted to. Rock and roll, finish the rest!

My friend Cindy has never heard any of my regressions. I don't let anyone listen to them as they make me very uncomfortable. However I did have to listen to them in order to write this book. I find it amazing how much Cindy's regression mirrors one of mine. Believe me when I say she could not have made this experience up unless she was engaged in the same nightmare I was.

Cindy's only regression took place on October 24, 2014. It took place in my apartment. It was the same place where four out of five of my regressions took place. Her husband dropped her off the day before because I wanted to make sure she was not under the influence of alcohol.

Cindy had been an alcoholic since we were teenagers. I wanted to make sure her mind was as clear as possible and we had discussed this at length before she arrived. It was imperative that she be sober. It was only one day, but it seemed to have been too much for her.

When she arrived, it was very obvious she had been drinking. She assured me she was fine. Unfortunately, these were the same words I had heard from her so many times in the past and the reason I had removed her from my life so many times.

I turned on a movie. However, she had great difficulty watching it through because she so frequently had to break to smoke a cigarette. Cindy easily smoked five packs a day. I became frustrated and decided to go to bed for the night. I left my bedroom window open that night because it was beautiful out. I left the television in my bedroom on so I wouldn't hear the patio doors open every time she wanted to smoke.

When I got up in the morning it was apparent that Cindy had not gotten any sleep, and she admitted to having found a bottle of vodka I had carefully hidden, and drinking it. I was livid with her, and told her that Vaughn likely would not even bother with her unless she got her shit together. My anger seemed to bring her to her senses because I knew how badly she wanted and needed this regression.

When Dr. Vowels arrived he spent a good amount of time speaking with her. I knew she would feel comfortable with Vaughn, as he is a very quiet and soft-spoken man with a natural calming effect. Cindy lay on the couch. I placed a pillow behind her head and covered her with a light afghan to make her more comfortable and relaxed. I listened to her breathing deepen and slow as Vaughn spoke softly and lead her to a place of total relaxation. I quietly placed my tape recorder behind her head and turned it on to record. Vaughn takes her back to that summer day and Cindy begins. She seems to be scanning the area even though her eyes are shut.

She began to relate where she was and what was going on.

I see my dad and a telescope. Nancy is there and my sister Kathy and my brothers. My neighbors are there. I see a saucer, and it's between my house and Nancy's. It is round, red, green, and silver. I am looking at it and wondering what it is. Nancy is yelling and screaming, "What is it? What is it?" My dad is so excited and everyone is in disbelief at what we are seeing. Nancy is yelling. It is like she is walking away and she is calling my name. I don't see Nancy anymore and I am wondering. It is getting dark and I knew she had to be home. I don't know when my dad called her dad. I don't know what they said. Nancy disappeared. I don't see her anymore, and the next thing I remember is being in a tube and seeing Nancy. I'm in the tube and I see Nancy and she is standing up and then she is lying down and they are doing something to her stomach and I am afraid they will do that to me. I saw them! Big eyes and almost skeleton-type looking but I don't feel afraid. I was afraid for Nancy but I don't feel afraid because I was in the tube so I felt like I was protected in that tube. But then I wondered if they were going to take me out and do to me what they were doing to Nancy. I don't remember speaking to Nancy in there. The only time I remember speaking to Nancy is before she disappeared yelling for me. Then I am in the tube. I am safe.

Vaughn asks Cindy how she got out of the tube, and Cindy replied, "I don't know how I got there, or how I got out."

154

Vaughn queried further, "What is the first thing you remember when you got out of the tube?"

Without hesitation, Cindy said, "I was home and my dad said he had talked to Nancy's dad and I believe, but I don't know, but I believe Nancy was home because it was past dark. I don't know if my dad called to see if she got home or if her dad called my dad. I just know there was a conversation between our fathers. My dad called people because he was excited and he swore it was a UFO."

"Do you remember what you said to your dad," Vaughn continued his line of questioning.

Once more, Cindy quickly replied, "I never told my dad I was in the tube, and I am trying to think of what I said. We talked about it for days and it was in the paper. It was a small town and everybody was talking about it. I believe my dad was worried about Nancy and her father was worried. It's coming to me now that my dad is telling me that I am okay. We were kids. My brother is jumping up and down. Everyone was excited. Anyone that saw it was excited. I know my neighbor and his kids were there and down the street people were outside."

Vaughn changes up the line of questioning a bit, and asks Cindy to open up and try and receive a message of why this contact with Nancy and Cindy.

There is silence for a few moments. Then she answers, "I believe Nancy needed me and I was there because she needed me. I felt like I had to be with her. I feel God wanted me to be with Nancy. But how could I leave Nancy? Why did I leave Nancy? I wish I could get that answer."

Vaughn then asks her if she thought her leaving was her willing it and if she felt she was still in control.

"I think I thought she was safe," Cindy replied, "I was scared of what they were doing to her and scared they were going to do it to me. But then I feel I knew Nancy was safe. Nancy didn't need me anymore because she told me she was safe."

"So, you were there for your friend," Vaughn comments, and asks Cindy if there are any other messages to help her gain clarity.

"I don't know how I got home safe," she said, "I knew Nancy was home safe but I don't know how I got there and back and where did my dad think I was? My dad would have been mad but he wasn't mad at me though. My dad was strict but kind of mellow. Not strict like Nancy's dad. They were completely different people."

Vaughn then asks Cindy to imagine her father is sitting next to her, and she can ask him any question about that day or any day, and to remember he is there, "He is with you."

Once again, Cindy did not hesitate with her answer. "I miss him and I know he was there and he put his arms around me; I didn't remember that! I even think he put his arms around Nancy. Nancy was screaming and my dad was trying to calm her down and it was almost like my dad was a second dad to her. I know my dad was concerned about her as he was concerned about me. I wasn't as hyper as Nancy was at that moment. I was calm like my dad. I was amazed and Nancy was so unbelievably scared and she was yelling and she knew 'they' were taking her and she didn't want to leave me and my dad. I know the phone was being used a lot. My dad went in the house and the neighbors were still out. I don't know if that is when my dad called Nancy's dad, but he was calming us down."

"Cindy," Vaughn continues, "I want you to imagine that you are with your father and he is in spirit form and he knows everything that has ever happened and he has all the knowledge of what happened that day and all the questions have been answered for him. He knows exactly what happened and he is going to tell you what he knows. Listen to him and let him tell you."

There was a drawn out silence. Then, Cindy begins to disclose the information her father was telling her in the trance.

"He believed and he followed this (the sighting) and he believed it was covered up by the government because it was in the paper and he saw it and they were calling him a liar. My dad is telling me what we saw was real, completely real. Believe that, this is real and this did happen to you and Nancy. He said there were two cars. Something stopped and there was a light that came down on Meadowbrook, on two cars." Then, Cindy begins to weep with heartfelt sadness, saying her father is concerned with her alcoholism. For the next several minutes that was the focus of the discussion, and the regression ended.

I was wiping back my own tears because at that moment I realize how much Cindy loves me and how guilty she felt for leaving me alone on the ship. She had carried that guilt for fifty-three years.

Cindy's husband, Doug Vandergriff, died a couple of months after her regression. He never, even for a single second, doubted either one of us. In fact, when I was at their house in April of 2012 (just before "they" took Drax), Cindy said something about my swollen stomach and I tried to laugh it off, telling her that Sid and I

156

were going to have a baby. Cindy laughed, but after I left their home, Doug told her I was pregnant. He knew!

So many times during these past four years I have wanted and tried to wash my hands of it all. I would become overwhelmed and exhausted. I would tell the Reptilians to leave me alone. I felt so lonely and isolated at times. I had few people I could share with, and they were not experiencers, so I felt totally frustrated and at times very angry. As far as family support I had only *one cousin*!

When I think about that now, I become infuriated. Today I have friends that refuse to listen to me or allow me to share because it makes them feel uncomfortable or scared.

I frequently think, "These are my friends?" They will change the subject or do whatever they have to so they do not have to listen to me. I suffered over and over again with bouts of depression and locked myself away from the world. Knowing this really upset my friends. They felt helpless watching me flounder over and over. They wanted to be supportive, and would take on the role of "mother or father", wanting to protect me or separate me from the Reptilians. They had trouble understanding their intentions and motives, as did I.

On December 17th I contacted one of my closest friends on Skype to tell her I was done with all of it and was tired of the roller coaster of emotions.

She replied, "I don't think 'they' should expect any different from you. It's all take and no give. They expect you to be willing, miserable, and a martyr. They don't understand the human spirit very well, or they are selfish and don't care."

I agreed, but was quick to remind her that every time I have these feelings to separate, "they" seem to reel me back in. They seem to take me to the brink of my tolerance and ability to cope, and then almost like a bribe or reward, they throw me a bone…

They will never let me go…

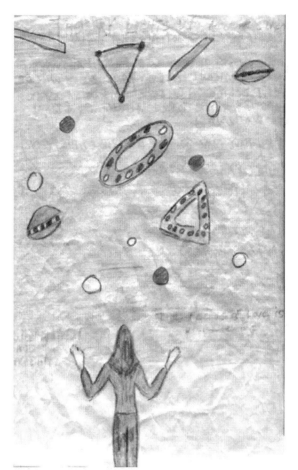

Feeling Elated at the Sight of the Ships

Chapter 12
The Book

True to form, the Reptilians would once again reel me back in, and once again I would be more than willing and ready to give it my all.

I wrote so many people that I don't even remember how I found Starborn Support because I cannot find anything in my sent emails from either Google or Yahoo. It was the best move I ever made.

For nearly four years I have reached out to everybody who was anybody in Ufology and to experiencers like myself. I was sure other experiencers would respond, but they did not. One woman's story so closely resembled mine that I thought she would be thrilled to have found someone of "like mind and kind." When she did not return my reaching out to her, I was heartbroken. I may have taken several breaks along the way, but nothing stopped me. I needed to be heard, and there was nothing that would stop me from speaking out. I had important information to share, and that the Reptilians wanted their messages and my stories out.

I received an email from Michael Austin Melton with Starborn Support Radio explaining how the program worked. He asked me if I was interested in doing a radio show. I couldn't believe that someone heard me and was actually willing to give me the opportunity to share my story.

On December 29, 2014, Michael called to discuss the radio interview. One of the very first things I said to him was that I was willing to take a lie detector test. He said it was not necessary and that I did not need to prove anything to him, and that every experiencer's story is unique, important and needs to be heard.

I assumed this was something he tells all of his guests, but I was determined that he was not going to have one single doubt when I was through with him. I gave him phone numbers of witness willing to speak on my behalf.

Vaughn Vowels, my regression therapist, sent Michael an email regarding my regressions and my credibility. He also agreed to call into the show and become part of the radio program. Tom, my friend of over twenty years, sent him an email explaining my effect on things electrical, and that he was a witness to my pregnancy with Drax. I gave him other names and numbers as well. I was given the option of remaining anonymous. I refused to entertain that idea, and I would be the owner of my story. Why add more mystery to the mysterious?

Cindy and I spoke at length, and I made it clear that she was to be sober when she called Michael the following morning as he was expecting her call. Once more I had put my faith in her and again she would allow alcohol to rule her life. When I called her the following evening I asked her how her conversation went with Michael. "Who," she asked. My heart started to race and my entire body shook with anger.

"Michael from the radio program!" I screamed, "He was expecting your call!"

"Oh," she said, "I overslept and forgot all about it. I'll call him now."

"No! Don't you dare," I screamed into the phone, "Don't call him, you hear me?" Of course, she ignored everything I said and called me later saying that she left a message on his answering machine. I was, and am still, embarrassed and I never mentioned her name again to Michael. This was the reason why, once again, I chose to distance myself from Cindy. I've not spoken a word to her since that conversation. I never realized how much I would regret this choice.

On January 24, 2015, I had my very first radio interview. I put my book aside and spent every minute getting prepared for the interview both mentally and emotionally.

A part of me knew I would have help from the Reptilians. This interview was the very first time in fifty-three years that I was given the opportunity to share my story and they wanted me to make sure I talked about my experiences in the greatest detail. For part of the time I spoke it felt like I was on automatic pilot.

Words seemed to come out of my mouth and I was hearing them for the first time, just like the "Listeners." It was such a healing process for me and so very overdue.

Michael and Julia Weiss, his co-host, and Jamie Havican, producer of the show, threw me a life jacket, and I grabbed it! It was the first time in my life I truly understood what it meant to feel humbled. That interview gave me the strength to continue on this journey. I know my true mission, and I know why I am here on this Earth.

After the interview a close friend wrote to me saying that she believed I had finally found the support I was looking for. "It sounds like they are going to direct you and put you in touch with the right people. You did a great job explaining your story. It is so tough to tell it all, but you did well."

She asked me if I had spoken with them after the show and I told her yes, and that I felt more love from them than from my own family. I told her they had asked me to do another interview in the future and I hoped this would give me the opportunity to do public speaking. I will always be grateful that she was the one that had the patience to teach me how to use a computer.

My cousin Chris was very proud of me for having the courage to share my story. He was impressed with the way Michael and I seemed to bounce off each other, and how nicely our voices blended.

On January 25th I received an email from Vaughn, and he wrote to me, "Your voice is beginning to be heard. Don't let anyone silence it. Landi must be proud of you, you are building on her legacy. It takes the courage of many to change the world."

I also got a message from "Mr." after the interview. The message was for Vaughn. Mr. wanted me to thank him for understanding my journey and my mission. He also asked that Vaughn remain in my life.

A few days later on the 29th I received a letter from the National Personnel Records Center telling me they did not have my father's military records, and that they were likely destroyed by the fire of July 12, 1973.

On the 9th of February I sent Michael an email telling him what a healing experience this has been for me. I also expressed my hopes that he would steer me in the right direction and help me to continue to get my story out.

However, the roller coaster ride was not always pleasurable. I found myself anxious to speak to everyone I met about my experiences. Of course I knew it was not a possibility and again I went back into my shell holding everything inside. I felt so alone and desperately wished I had someone in my life to share everything with.

I felt like I was totally alone in this journey. It is true I have a few friends, but they have their own lives and their own relationships and they are not able to be there (nor do I expect them to be...) to comfort me in the middle of the night when the "high strangeness" creeps into my slumber and into my room. They would not be able to understand and they certainly would not "get it" anyway so I didn't even consider it an option.

Vaughn Vowels once told me that it would be very difficult – if not impossible to have a relationship with someone who was not an experiencer or in the field of abduction research, or someone very knowledgeable and actively interested in the subject.

So many times I just wanted to pack a suitcase, and jump into my car and drive. Just drive to wherever the road takes me to get as far away from all of this as is humanly possible. I pray and beg for Mr. to come and take me. I feel so unattached to this planet, and not a part of this reality at all, as strange as that might sound.

On February 20th of 2015 I sent Michael Austin Melton an email:

Hi, Michael,

I am crying as I write these words. I should be excited that my story is getting out, and I was, I really was. Then reality set in as I realized that I have absolutely no one to share with. I have no family or friends that understand. Only people I have never met can grasp my reality. The solitude is crippling. I am in such a depression that I am unable to, and have no desire to work on my book. I see that other experiencers have relationships and people they can share with, and I envy them. The solitude, the solitude… The solitude…

Michael promptly replied:

Hi, Nancy!

I would recommend that you get involved in the work being done to bring about recognition to persons like yourself. I am going to give you some phone numbers and I want you to call. There is a lot of fulfillment in simply doing some of the reach out work, and I know you would be excellent at it. You've got a kind heart and more than a lifetime of experience to share. Nancy, there is no need to feel alone. Call me if you need any help. I am always here for you, Nancy.

On February 22nd I emailed Michael again:

Hi Michael, I spent three days reaching out for help. I was losing it. Today (author) Erica Goetsch called me and as I was talking with her another call came in and it was Bridget Smith, all this while I was instant messaging with Miesha Johnston! Talk about timing!

Mr. must have realized I was suffering too much and took pity on me. I received this message from him: "In regards to your question what is at the end of the road, the answer is 'Home.'" "Yes, yes!" I shouted. Now I had another question. 'What does 'home' mean? Where is 'home?' and what is 'home?'" My questions for the Reptilians never end, and neither do their answers.

I sent Michael an email asking him if he would read the first two chapters of my book and tell me what he thought. I had only shared these chapters with a couple of people and needed the advice of a professional. He told me he would be glad to. I explained to him how hard it was for me to ask others for help.

On March 8, 2015, I sent Michael the first two chapters of my book. I anxiously awaited his critique. He offered to do some editing and send them back to me. I was thrilled!

He told me he thought my story would be of interest to many. I told him I would love him to do the editing, and I wanted him to be the first to read my chapters as I wrote them. I knew Michael was one of the "meant-to-be" people I would meet along the path of my journey. Over the course of the next couple of days I sent Michael the third and fourth chapters and I was also trying to figure out a way to ask Michael to be part of this journey.

On March 23rd Michael is now on board and official editor of my book. I gave Michael the title of the book that was given to me by Mr., "*Symbiosis.*"

This word perfectly describes my relationship with the Reptilians: "Two species dependent on each other or the interaction between two organisms living in close physical association, typically to the advantage of both. "

Michael's feedback had now become crucial, and I needed his advice on every decision regarding the book. He liked the title, and also mentioned the idea of bringing David Chace on board to do the cover, and any other color illustrations the book required.

I had seen some of David's work and jumped at the idea. Michael also called me out about talking about my father in the book, but that I barely ever mentioned my mother.

I replied, "You noticed I skipped over my childhood. Hey, you're pretty good, Michael." I promptly sent David Chace a request to do the cover for the book. He accepted, and Michael and I were both very pleased. What an adventure we are on.

On April 14, 2015 Michael asked if he could soften some of my description regarding some of my heightened sexual abilities from the tuning of my pineal gland. I knew I had been overly graphic, but the women I have spoken to have not understood and even the doctors and nurses were not able to comprehend or believe what was happening to me. If doctors and nurses couldn't understand, how could the average person? I don't even understand it! In the end I won out and my words and descriptions were left as they were written. I will not change my life to make others comfortable.

On May 28th I sent Michael my illustrations. I had considered hiring an artist to redo my illustrations as mine for the most part look like a child drew them. I even sent him a new one that the Reptilians wanted me to include – "The Fear Challenge." I am pleased now that my original illustrations will be used for the book because they are mine and no one else would be able to capture the emotions contained within each one.

Michael wrote back upon receiving them thanking me and acknowledging that he understood how difficult it was for me to share these sketches. He also wanted to discuss another radio interview. He called it "Part Two." We agreed on a date, and thus scheduled it for June 6, 2015. I asked Michael to refer to me as an experiencer rather than an abductee. An abductee is taken against their will. Instead, I am a very willing experiencer and participant.

My June 6th appearance on Starborn Support Radio did not go as smoothly as my first appearance did. I was too focused and wrapped up in writing this book. There was just too much on my mind, and I was having trouble concentrating. It was due to emotional overload and the fact that I was told not to go in depth regarding my sexual experiences.

I ended up freezing up a couple of times and felt like a deer in the headlights. Julia, co-host of the radio show, knew instinctively to come to my rescue and filled enough time for me to gather my senses.

My regressions were brought up as subject matter and I was not prepared to address them. Unless I have my notes regarding my regressions I am lost and unable to remember them as I must put forth a lot of effort to overcome the mental blocks I set in place to protect myself.

I was also most displeased with the way I handled the pineal manipulation and the hospital visits. This is such an important part of my story, and something that I lived with for over a year. I was unable to use the words "orgasm" and "ejaculation."

I realized just how much damage the doctors and nurses did to me by making me feel dirty and ashamed of something I had no control over. I was begging for their help, and they laughed at me. They used everything and every medical test to prove me wrong. In the end, I was victorious. Truth always wins out.

Why is it not shameful to show beheadings, murder and police brutality, tortured animals and explicit and violent television shows, and not be able to discuss female sexuality, orgasms and ejaculation?

Why does this cause so much discomfort for others? Something is very wrong here. Society has made a wrong turn somewhere. In the future, when speaking, I will not be embarrassed to use those words. I did nothing wrong in describing my experiences and am not ashamed.

Even though I was very displeased with my second interview, I received very positive feedback. The next day, June 7th, Vaughn sent me an email.

He told me, "Excellent night on KGRA. I really enjoyed the show and everyone's contribution to the subject of our ETs purposes on Earth. You are part of the most important (Earth shattering) development in our evolution. Keep up the courageous work. I am very happy to know that the support network with Starborn Radio is there for one another. You've found a home away from home."

I sent Michael chapter 10 telling him I had a long way to go and might possibly have to add another chapter. He responded, telling me how proud he was and he encouraged me to keep writing. He also reminded me that if things got difficult I could call him at any time. Michael has been my rock.

Reflecting on the whole process I was part of, I realized how much more difficult it is for me to get the Reptilians message out. It is not like they are the Nordics or Tall Blondes.

When I am talking to people and say the words "Reptilian race," or "Draconian Reptilians," people immediately imagine a stinky, scaly creature. When I thought to myself how difficult they had made this journey for me, I was immediately interrupted and given the message "Beauty is in the *heart* of the beholder."

I no longer see their physical form. They communicate with me using what they call "Light Knowledge Energy." We have moved beyond the need of physical. I am again reminded of a message received years earlier, "no matter what we are, we are always who we are."

On June 15th to my surprise I received a phone call from the woman who responded to my Novi News article back in October of 2013 regarding the 1961 event that marked the beginning of my involvement with the Reptilians. She still wanted to remain anonymous and I will always respect that wish. No longer did she speak in a whispering tone, and she spoke clearly about what she remembered, and she was quick to state that she had ample time to reflect on the incident. A few of her memories had changed since our first conversation. The time of the incident had changed by several hours, as she was now inside her bedroom when she saw the ship coming at her. She said she believed the ship was actually watching her, but was quick to rationalize that statement by saying that could not have been possible unless the ship was telepathic. She said she tried to scream because it was coming right at her, but was unable because she was paralyzed. She was able to sleep for a few hours after the sighting, but does not understand how that was possible since she was terrified. She added a new detail to her story: Her father had called Mettetal Airport located near Novi the following morning to ask if there had been any strange sightings reported, and of course there had not been any reported. Mettetal airport covers an area of approximately sixty-three acres and has only one runway. Commercial airlines are not permitted access to this field.

Her thoughts concerning hypnotic regression had drastically changed as well. The first time we spoke she would not consider regression as an option for herself. Now, even though she still believes she was never aboard the craft, she now considers hypnotic regression a possible course of action. She also claims to have spoken to her husband about the event, and he believes her. She figured the distance between our homes was about eight miles.

What never changed from her report is the triangular shape of the UFO, and that it was completely silent as it hovered above the trees. She also validated that a beam of light came out of the bottom of the craft, and we agreed that the event occurred during the summer of 1961. After we talked, I came to the conclusion that our sightings might have been two separate events that occurred during that summer. I am also aware that UFOs can alter their size and shape. When necessary the occupants can manipulate time as well, therefore, I rule nothing out. As I mentioned in the beginning of this book, "The more I know, the less I know." Now, in this very chapter, I am writing this book in real time. I am no longer writing about past memories – we now move to the present. I am writing about events that are occurring in real time.

On June 29 2015, I was Googling "Chief BeGole" checking for an obituary. After all, it had been several months since we had spoken, and my phone calls were never returned. To my surprise, not only was Chief BeGole alive and well, but the Novi Rotary club was hosting his 95th birthday party – a surprise one at that. The party was on the 2nd of July, just three days away!

Had I not Googled him that very day, I would have missed out on another opportunity to see the chief. I immediately called the phone number listed and asked to be put on the guest list.

Police chief BeGole's birthday party was only two or three blocks away from where the major sighting was in 1961. I decided to drive past my childhood home and stare at the area where I had seen the ship. The area just down the street from my home is now named The City of Novi Parkland, and it is regulated wetlands and woodlands to be maintained in a natural and undeveloped condition.

The officials who supervise this property are from both The City of Novi and Michigan Department of Natural Resources & Environment. It is the area that we as children called "Man Made Lake," and where we used to ice skate as kids. It is also the area where Cindy and I both, independent of one another, believed that was the lake the UFO used for regenerating power and hiding.

It is July 2, 2015. On that day I arrived 15 minutes early and entered the main room to find that all the tables in the front of the room were filled. This was Retired Chief BeGole ninety-fifth birthday. I asked if I might seat myself, and I was told to sit anywhere I pleased. I chose one of the empty tables, and the first person said to me, "I know you! I work at the Novi library." "Yes," I answered, "You helped me go through the archives." Another woman came to sit at the table. Her nametag read "Kathy Mutch." I spoke of her in the last chapter. Chief BeGole had given me her name as the current Novi historian. I mentioned to her I had tried to call her several times, and that her phone went immediately to her answering machine. She told me she had been very ill, and was in long-term care for a good while. Shortly thereafter a man, his wife, and his mother joined me. The man's wife asked me how I knew Chief BeGole, and I told her my family and I moved to Novi in the mid-1950s. Denise, told me that she too had lived in Novi all of her life. She was a few years younger than I. I asked her if she remembered the Schingeck family, and she immediately mentioned one of my brothers. She told me her maiden name was Ward, and I immediately said "David!" David was her cousin. Then, taking a big risk, I asked her if she remembered a UFO sighting that occurred in Novi in 1961. She did! I nearly jumped out of my seat. I asked her what she remembered. She said, "I was only nine, but I remember people talking about it." "Yes," I replied. "I told her about a woman on Facebook who talked about a UFO sighting in the very same spot in the 1970s."

We hit it off, and I explained to her how important it was for me to get a photo of Chief BeGole and me for my book. She promised to arrange it for me. I would have that picture after the party. There never seemed to be an opportunity to talk to the chief because people continuously surrounded him. Chief BeGole's surprise party drew over ninety people. He was loved and respected by many. I scanned the room for familiar faces and noticed that the event photographer was John Heider, the same person that did the video for the Novi News. I spoke with him for a few minutes telling him I was working on writing a book, and mentioned that I had kept in touch with BeGole over the years. He did not seem surprised.

Now, it began to get very strange. One of the speakers was retired police Captain Dick Faulkner. I recognized the name as one of Cindy's ex-husband's older brothers. Cindy and I had lost touch when she was married to this man. I recall her mentioning to me later on that one of her brother-in-law's brothers was a former Novi police officer, but she was not sure if he was a police officer back in 1961. Faulkner sure looked old enough, so I approached him and asked him if he would be willing to speak with me when he had a couple of minutes. He was all smiles and said he had time right then. I opened up the conversation that my friend Cindy had been married to his older brother.

He let out a groan of disdain and I realized that I had touched on a sore spot. He made a distasteful remark. I regretted mentioning her name, but I was too deep into this conversation to simply abandon it now. I asked him if he was a police officer in 1961, and all I got was a steely glare and a "Yes." I asked him if he remembered the sighting in 1961. With a condescending tone he asked, "What sighting?" I said, "You know, the UFO sighting."

He forced what was clearly a phony laugh as he said, "I have no idea what you are talking about." I challenged him and said, "Well, Chief BeGole and Martin Cone remembered it." I got another icy glare as he turned and walked away. He said nothing! I stood there watching him make his way back to his seat. I was embarrassed and pissed off. How could he be so rude and why didn't he say he would ask BeGole, or at least call me "crazy?"

The birthday cake was finally served, and several speakers took turns sharing stories about this beloved chief. It was obvious how much he affected so many people's lives. There is now a street named after him, and his home is now a historic sight. I believe that demonstrates how much he means to the city of Novi, Michigan. The chief spoke for several minutes and had the audience laughing as he shared many of his memories with humor and great compassion. His mind was very clear that day, and I assumed his memory was in good working order. After the closing remarks from the Rotary president many of the people approached BeGole to shake his hand, and then leave. My new friend Denise and I waited for the right moment to approach the chief, and after all of the photos had been taken I approached him, recorder in hand.

"Hey!" I called out, "I'm Nancy Tremaine, the woman you have been talking to for the last four years." I mentioned the UFO incident, and he immediately told me he had not forgotten our conversations, and that he is still working on it (the sighting data). I look up, and guess who is standing right behind the chief – Officer Faulkner! He is giving me dirty looks, and staring at my recorder like it was a loaded pistol. BeGole mentions the word UFO, and Officer Faulkner breaks into our private conversation, "No, I don't remember it…UFO?" He chuckled and then slapped BeGole on the back and said, "You shot it down, didn't ya, chief?" He looked right into my eyes and said, "We buried it." It was obvious to me at that moment he was no longer referring to the UFO. He was alluding to the supposed fact that the topic had now been buried. He was not fooling me – Faulkner remembered. After all, the chief told me after that sighting the whole police station was buzzing with and about news of the saucer.

Several minutes later, I found another chance to approach BeGole with my recorder. I started the conversation, "Are you living in Novi?"

My house is still there," he answers, "But I have a home in Detroit."

"Chief," I told him with concern, "You are all I have left."

"I am working on it," He reassures me, "You know, I am having a hard time. How did you know about this party today? I didn't even know about it!" I certainly was not going to tell him that I found the party announcement while I was searching for his obituary. I said, "Oh, the same way I found you the last time in 2011 for the street signing: by accident. Someone up above is trying to get you to give me the answers I am searching for."

The chief bends forward, as if to tell me a secret, and says, "We are the only ones that know anything about it, and that is, and I mean, the story."

Chief BeGole and Nancy

"Why don't you tell anybody about it," I asked.

"I do! I'll tell them," looking around nervously he continued, "I just found out today that one of my long-time officers didn't even remember it."

"Yes," I related, "I approached him and he treated me like I was crazy." Looking surprised, he asked, "Who was that?"

"That was Dick Faulkner," I said.

"Faulkner?" He said with a look of surprise," He was on the job that day! Did you mention Marty Cone to him?"

"Yes," I answered.

"Did he recognize it then?" The chief asked.

"No." I said.

Shaking his head, BeGole sighed long and drawn out, "Oh... well."

"Your memory is better than his," I said with a smile. We both laughed. Then, for a second time the chief voiced the words, "He was on the job that day."

This is something no one would ever be able to forget. "I can't forget," Chief BeGole added, "I got these calls from my own patrol car. When Don Young's wife called, I told her yes, we know all about it and a car is on its way, so there is nothing wrong with your mind!"

After all the festivities, I went home to do some research on Faulkner. I discovered he is now seventy-nine years old, which would have made him twenty-six years old in 1961. Could he be the officer whose arm I tugged on and asked, "Is this real?"

While I was at the party, Denise took a couple of pictures of me and BeGole." I struck up a conversation with a woman whose name was Annie. She drove the chief to the party, and was patiently waiting on him. She told me she had met the chief many years ago and they became friends. She told me she helped him out with driving, and cleans for him occasionally.

I explained my situation as best as I could, and told her that somewhere in his home the files from 1961 were collecting dust. BeGole told me himself that he never threw anything out, and believed he had his own complete set of records.

I begged her to please not throw anything out and stressed how critical it is to get hold of these papers. I will continue to call the chief and his friend Annie. Who knows what the future holds? A few weeks ago I was ending the book with chapter eleven. Now, I am trying to end it with chapter twelve, but anything could happen today or tomorrow before I get a chance to ship it off to Michael for editing.

Next month I will meet Michael for the first time in Portland, Maine at the Experiencers Speak conference for 2015. Michael helped make this book possible. He believed in me and he believed I have an important story to tell, and he has given me this opportunity to share it. From Mr., the Reptilians and me, I thank you, Michael.

My internal struggles with the Reptilians continue to this day. Like any relationship, it has its good and bad aspects, days, and events. It seems this is the only relationship I have ever been willing to work at.

Since this journey began in 2011 I have kept track of every event in my life. I have recorded all important phone calls, kept all emails, took videos and pictures of all the "high strangeness" events,

I have drawn illustrations for nearly four years from memories and mental images the Reptilians have provided me, along with their personal and important messages. I have recordings of three out of my five regressions as well as one regression of Cindy who was on board the ship with me in 1961.

I have hospital records that prove all tests performed on me came back normal. Not one doctor could find anything out of the ordinary. I had an MRI, an EKG, an EEG and a sleep study. I even have a copy of the disc that supposedly showed I had a heart attack. They performed a heart catheterization and it proved I had a perfectly healthy heart. Dr. Steele, who performed the procedure, stated that only a miracle could explain this.

I would love for an independent cardiologist take a look at this X-Ray chest view. Even my cholesterol was perfect. The neurological report states "alert and oriented to person, time and situation." Bottom line is that there is *nothing wrong* with me, and I have all the hospital records to prove it. Yes, there will be debunkers, and I welcome them! They haven't met Laveet*! I am strong, persistent, and I want to leave a stain on this planet!*

Cindy

While Michael and I were diligently working on this book, one of the most important people in my life passed away. On August 3, 2015, I awoke from a terrible nightmare about someone I loved dearly dying.

I was screaming in the nightmare, and no sound was coming out of my mouth. I sat up in bed and began to cry uncontrollably. I felt no one could console me, the way I felt at that moment.

The next day, August 4th, I went to visit my friend Tom so he could print out my airline tickets and hotel reservation for the Experiencers Speak 2015 conference, only a few weeks away.

We were going to take some time to order some business cards, but he was called to duty from his second job, and our time was unfortunately cut short that day. While I was visiting him, I happened to mention that I had not heard from Cindy for a while, and said, partly in jest and partly in concern, "She is probably dead."

Well, she was dead. Cindy would call me every week, and sometimes twice in the same week leaving me messages that she loved me, and in one message said that she was sorry for not calling Michael. I really hoped that my punishment of ignoring her and not returning her calls would cause her to stop drinking.

The morning of August 5th was like any other. I got up like I do every day and jumped onto the net to Facebook. Cindy's niece is on my friend's list, and I began to read her post. She referred to August 4th in her post. "Yesterday, my post about my Aunt Cindy was needing to home her dog immediately; and she is a sweetie. But those who know me well, know that I've taken my mom's sister shopping, and if I couldn't get there I spoke with her weekly, if not more to check in. She was an alcoholic. She is someone whose head shakes because she needs more. Not just someone who drinks daily but someone who falls all the time, and drinks in parking lots and stores. She wanted to quit over and over..."

At that point, I couldn't read any further. I called my friend Tom crying hysterically. I was overcome with emotion and guilt. I kept repeating over and over, "Cindy is dead! Cindy is dead... and I am reading about it right now on Facebook and I can't read it alone, and I can't hear these words alone. Please hear them with me. I will read them, and we will hear them together." Through my tears I continued to read.

"...She did succeed a few times. I spoke with her last week and she said she quit and we talked for quite a while (she didn't). She grieved the loss of my mom very hard. Then, to lose her husband. She drank even more after that. Sadly, seeing someone this way is not an easy thing, but my mom always told me 'Aunt Cindy has to help herself.' She lived in a not so nice area of Detroit where her friend came by to check on her and peeked into the window and saw her on the floor and she had to have been passed for two or three days.

Poor Lucy (her dog). As quickly as Cindy's body was taken out the looters came. Not kidding. Everyone was outside waiting to get into her house. Like sharks. I swear, my husband couldn't believe it. The police left the door off and had her friend guard the house until we got there with more family. Just crazy, and honestly this is part of the reason over the last three years I barely drank.

Seeing someone like this honestly makes you hate it. My guess is she had a heart attack and fell face first and I bet she was on a long binge (like six months of intoxication). We will miss her.

Alivia (Cindy's niece) was very upset when I told her. She picked Lucy (Cindy's dog) out and saw Aunt Cindy the most. After I told her through her tears she said, 'Mom, when people drink it makes them want more, it's not their fault, they can't help it. Just like how she smoked, the cigarettes made her want more.' Wise words from a ten year old."

That was the end of her post. The next day, August 6th, I went for a walk behind my apartment. Tears streamed down my face from behind my sunglasses, and I went from grief to anger as I started to yell and swear at Cindy.

I shouted, "Damn you, I will never forgive you for this. This was our story and I wanted you to stand next to me in front of an audience and speak. Now, I have no one!"

Astonishingly, I received these words from Cindy, "I can help you. Someone has to work from behind the scenes." Then she said, "Those men..." and I knew exactly what men she was referring to.

She continued, "...they came to your house, they wanted to talk to you, and your dad threatened to kill them." There was my answer to why my father went to California after the incident. Those sick bastards wanted to talk to a twelve-year-old child? I believe Cindy will be with me as long as I need her. I know she will. Below is a picture of the two of us in the 80s.

Nancy and Cindy

Chapter 13
The Psychology of the Experiencer: The Inside and the Outside

by Michael Austin Melton

Experiencer Nancy Tremaine is a dynamic, lively and lovely lady, and, I can honestly say, a good friend of mine. Assisting her in the editing of this book has given me the impression that I have known her all of her life. There is not one word of fiction in this story, and not one ounce of embellishment.

This book is Nancy Tremaine in the "raw." It is her truth. Her outgoing personality is addicting, and she is a pleasure to be around. However at the same time, she holds within her memory and in her present state a lifetime of hiding, ostracism, anxiety (PTSD), and fear.

Although the fear has subsided for the most part, she still suffers from many of the symptoms of post-traumatic stress. Had she not found the courage to write this book in the most intimate way, the story of her amazing life and the events contained therein would never have been heard, let alone understood.

Nancy's story is a very accurate example of the life of an experiencer. It is one story amongst many others. Thousands of men and women live the life Nancy does. If you are an experiencer, reading this book will give you a sense of not being alone attempting to manage the stigma of being an Abductee or Contactee.

It will help you to understand you are not a victim despite the negative aspects. If you are a "non-experiencer," by reading this book you will have been given the opportunity to take in and begin to understand the life of an experiencer.

It is an intimate journey into the life of one person who exists with terrorizing images and memories, recollections of examinations, and in Nancy's case, two pregnancies via alien in-vitro fertilization, and one normally conceived with a human male.

Perhaps the phenomenon of abduction by aliens becomes more real for you, the non-experiencer, as your understanding is increased. Maybe you will decide to recommend the book to others in the hopes their insight grows as well. Either way, you will be made more aware of what is happening.

Perhaps it's the biggest news in history. It is my personal belief that in the beginning, God created the heavens and the home we live on – The Earth. However, regardless of your belief system, you cannot deny the scope of this universe, perhaps one of millions that exist in different dimensions separate from us. The idea that the rest of creation is barren is a very naive one to say the least.

In space and time, inseparably woven together, there are other intelligent entities here, there, and everywhere, in different planes of existence, on different timelines, and/or inside different vibrational levels. As a matter of fact, I believe the various universes are teeming with life of all kinds and they are all over the place, and as I indicated; *they are certainly here*.

There is no doubt the world is changing around us. One only needs to watch CNN or even their local news to gain an understanding of those changes. Most of the changes are not at all pretty, and they give us a sense that the future is going to be anything but peaceful coexistence and prosperity.

However, there is a hint of change in the air – a hope that lies within certain very special individuals who might potentially be able to change the world we live in. Now, we have what we refer to as the "experiencer," which is a catch-all term meaning anyone who has been involved in alien abduction, anyone who has been in contact with entities from out of this world or out of this dimension or timeline, and it also includes those persons who have witnessed entities who came from an unidentified flying object, or a portal, involving either time or dimension, but who have not had contact (via any modality) with said entities; in other words, just observation only.

Who are these people who, like Nancy, have experienced something so bizarre and strange that they lost sight of how the world works, how they fit in with other people, who question what they believe in, and who feel alone and ostracized and labeled "crazy" by the society in which they exist?

Why would these individuals come forward with such a story that they would risk everything: reputation, employment, family and friends, acceptance, love and companionship and more, because they feel the need to "get it out of their system" or "get it off their chests" so they can move on with their lives?

I can tell you that they are average people. They are from all walks of life, rich and poor, homebound or homeless, employed or jobless, married or single, and the list goes on and on. Nancy Tremaine is one of these people.

Her interaction with the Reptilian race started early in life. Being somewhat different than your average abductee, but similar to others of her ilk, she discovered a practicality and purpose to her abductions and interaction with aliens.

That does not mean she skipped out on all of the negative aspects most experiencers go through – absolutely not! Nancy has suffered the loss of friends and family, independence, failed marriages, rejection, and became the person others steer clear of because of her honesty and openness and need to, like all the others, "get it out of her system" so life can be more "normal," whatever normal means as it is a relative term. She still, however, and despite all of this, carries on with her life, with meaning and a purpose that keeps her going day to day.

So, once again, who are these people we call "experiencers?" In my opinion, experiencers are very special people indeed, and *need to be seen and heard.* Each experiencer, by the very nature of their being in the presence of otherworldly beings, having been inside their flying machines or inter-dimensional craft, interacting with them, and many other factors, hold vital information inside them.

Call it a piece of the puzzle, or a way we can become a better race of people for having listened to what these experiencers have to tell us and learning what our alien visitors want to teach us.

Without referring to these entities as "gods," and instead thinking of them as explorers, seekers, who like us, want to know if *they* are alone in the universe, by listening we may advance ourselves such that we might raise ourselves above the need to go to war, or to kill each other…

Some of you might think that what I am proposing is naïve, and that I am foolishly optimistic. I tell you, it is not so! Consider the saying "as above, so below." There is good and evil everywhere.

Having been a "doom and gloom" conspiracy theorist in the past, I have since turned in my Armageddon membership card. The evil doom and gloom have not disappeared – I have chosen now to focus on the positive possibilities. It is just as meaningful to say, "Our extraterrestrial explorers are here with good intentions," as it is to say, "The aliens are here to hybridize the whole human race and take over the world!" So remember: as above, so below. They might both be correct, and likely are.

Take a closer look at Nancy's experiences, and you will see that optimism shining through. Her encounters and experiences amount to nothing worse than a symbiotic relationship consisting of learning, emotion, affection, and intention.

In exchange for the knowledge and "cultural" experiences Nancy receives, she gives the Draconian Reptilians a lesson in human emotion from terror to erotic, fear to assertiveness, and ignorance to empathy. Nancy describes her relationship with the Reptilian named "Mr." as a loving, caring, and almost parental one. Yet, she experienced the terror.

Recall the three tanks with a sea creature in each, capable of consuming Nancy in a single swallow. She came to no harm, and she was told she would never have been allowed to go near those tanks.

She experienced the extremes of passion and pleasure, a period of time that was physically gratifying, but mentally quite confusing and confounding. Understand that learning is confusing and confounding sometimes, and we misconstrue the facts, fail to understand the obvious but eventually come through the difficulties and walk away with our embossed paper degree.

I must admit that Nancy's life story has truly awakened the optimism I now experience. It has completely changed my view of the Reptilian race, and opened up my mind to understand that these alien visitors are indeed explorers and as far as the positive outlook can be understood, they mean us no harm, but are still what we call "human," for lack of a better term, meaning they can and do make mistakes, bad decisions, faulty plans, but in the long run, are not out to obliterate us – at least not in obvious ways.

Let's turn the tables a bit and examine the darker side of Nancy's experiences and how they might be understood. One could easily conclude that Nancy has lived a life of delusion and these reptilians are really out to consume her, body and soul.

They have put her through a disconcerting, disturbing and shameful experience throughout her life, and did nothing but drain her of her energies, Because of all this maltreatment she is now suffering from a "Stockholm Syndrome," a form of traumatic bonding we generally know involves a hostage or hostages.

However, hostages are not vital to the syndrome. It has been described as "strong, emotional ties that develop between two persons where one person intermittently harasses, threatens, abuses, or intimidates the other (Dutton & Painter, 1981)." It is obvious reading about Nancy's life that there certainly was a degree of this kind of manipulation. However, can we conclude Stockholm Syndrome if Nancy, at twelve years old stood on the head of her bed staring out of the window into the night sky asking for her abductors to return and take her with them? It's hard to say, but again, I am going to approach the entire concept from a positive mindset.

Working on this book with Nancy has been an adventure. When you edit a work of nonfiction, the story of someone's life, you feel a part of that life and you feel like a lifelong friend who has been a personal confidant.

I guess you might say it is just another relationship based on trust – a symbiosis! Thank you, Nancy, for allowing me to assist you in getting this story out to the thousands and thousands of experiencers who will benefit from reading this book. And last, but certainly not least, thank you Mr., for your trust in my abilities to help produce this work.

Chapter 14
UFOs, Reptilians, and the Context of Nancy's Experience

by David W. Chace

The UFO phenomenon has been with us for a long time, though the modern era is usually defined as having begun in 1947. During the first few decades following 1947, many types of UFO occupants were described.

Many of those were "one-offs" or known from only a few cases. In addition, there were a number of reports of human-looking beings, and of generic humanoids with large heads and prominent eyes (today known as "Grays").

There were isolated sightings of reptilians as far back as the sixties and seventies, but they really didn't become an accepted category of UFO occupant until the late eighties and early nineties, when researchers such as Barbara Bartholic, Dr. Karla Turner, and John Carpenter started speaking about them.

So what is a reptilian? Let's define our terms here. For our purposes, a reptilian is an alien (extraterrestrial, UFO occupant, etc...) or a cryptid (scientifically unrecognized creature) with a more or less humanoid body plan and a reptilian appearance. In general, a reptilian is defined in terms of its physical characteristics and/or similarities to other reported reptilians.

Research into the subject of reptilians is thus dependent on obtaining detailed physical descriptions and/or drawings of the aliens/cryptids reported by witnesses, to determine which ones fall into the reptilian category.

What constitutes a "reptilian appearance"? Skin covered with scales (variously described), facial features reminiscent of a lizard or snake, and fingers tipped with lizard-like claws are some of the most common identifying characteristics.

Other characteristics, such as webbed hands, eyes with vertical slit pupils and a bright yellow iris, or a muscular build and an overall height close to seven feet, recur in many cases, so they are also defining features.

"Mr." is a fairly typical reptilian as far as his anatomy is concerned. He is brownish green in color and covered with snake-like scales. He has golden irises with vertical slit pupils, and a long tail that rests on the floor (some reptilians have tails and some do not). Nancy does not recall a central forehead ridge, which a majority of reptilians seem to have.

Mr. also has visible "whites" in his eyes, which many reptilians do not. His build is somewhat muscular, and he is tall, in the seven to eight foot range. His hands are webbed, with three fingers and a thumb. The webbing extends perhaps to the first knuckle. He has webbed feet that resemble the feet of an alligator. He has claws on his hands and feet. Mr.'s nose is nearly flat (in the sense that a lizard's nose is "flat") and his mouth is a slit.

I knew that in order to put Nancy's reptilian experience in a larger context, I would have to write about sex. The experiences of many reptilian contactees attest to the fact that reptilians are sexual beings, like us, and have an interest not just in the creation of human-reptilian hybrids, but in human sexuality itself.

A number of people have spoken to me privately about this aspect of their contact with reptilians, but relatively few have wanted to be named publicly. Out of sensitivity to that, I will speak in general terms about some of what has been reported.

In the early nineties cases of rape by reptilians were some of the first cases I heard. It didn't paint the reptilians in a positive light. They had domineering personalities, and didn't seem to care what the experiencer wanted or did not want.

Over time, however, a more positive side to the issue of sexual contact with reptilians came to light. This was thanks in large part to one particular experiencer, a female jazz singer who had previously had typical "hybridization" type experiences with the Grays, but who, in 1996, went on national television to speak about having sex with a reptilian.

During her interview, she described the experience as "probably the best sex I ever had." Of course, given the sensationalistic nature of media reporting on paranormal topics, some of the coverage of her experience amounted to "sexual sound bites taken out of context."

There were some in the UFO community who found her report implausible, and felt that it detracted from what they regarded as more serious issues regarding UFO sightings and abductions. Nevertheless, she was genuine, articulate, and courageous, and by putting this aspect of the phenomenon on the table, she helped many other contactees who were beginning to become aware that they were in a sexual relationship with a reptilian.

Beyond the quality and intensity of her experience, the jazz singer spoke of the fact that she felt love from her reptilian mate. His purpose was not to frighten or dominate her, but seemed to be something more loving and benevolent.

Many reptilian contactees, particularly those who have a special relationship with a particular reptilian, have picked up, through intuition, dreams, and information brought forth in hypnotic regression, that this particular reptilian is someone they knew in a past life, possibly even a mate. By returning to them in this life the reptilian is simply continuing the relationship.

One such person is Miesha Johnston, a lifelong experiencer who runs an experiencer support group in Las Vegas. She has been repeatedly visited by a reptilian who asked that she refer to him as Iyano.

On one occasion, Iyano came into her boyfriend's body during love making, but as soon as Miesha realized it, she told him to leave his body. Iyano apologized and said he just wanted to feel what it would be like to be with her again.

Reptilians have an "energy" about them that experiencers can sense, both psychically and physiologically in their bodies. I have heard multiple reports from female contactees who have experienced sexual arousal when a familiar reptilian male came to them, even when he was in a dematerialized or "inter-dimensional" state.

There is something about the presence of a reptilian that can enable a person in their fifties or sixties to perform like they were in their twenties again, though it should be noted that reptilians are not the only type of alien who seem to be able to affect people in this way.

Some reptilian contactees have been visited in the astral (i.e., the out-of-body state), not only by reptilians, but apparently by other humans. For instance, there have been cases in which an apparently human man in an astral state attempted to seduce or rape a contactee. Astral encounters can sometimes leave physical marks, and a person in an astral state can sometimes physically interact with a person in the flesh.

Reptilians often take the role of teacher or protector. A number of reptilian contactees have been encouraged to speak a reptilian language, sometimes referred to as a star language or light language, as part of their contacts.

182

Vivid dreams of past lives or of parallel lives, as well as precognitive dreams, are sometimes reported by reptilian contactees. Clairvoyance and out-of-body travel are common psychic experiences reported by reptilian contactees.

One objection to accepting the reptilians, and other UFO occupants, as part of the objective physical world (even if a transient part, given their seeming "inter-dimensional" nature) is the hybridization issue.

Any biologist can tell you that a human should not be able to successfully reproduce with a humanoid reptile, let alone with an extraterrestrial being.

It is a similar situation with the apparently nonhuman Grays and their hybridization program. It is often assumed in ufology that the aliens get around such reproductive incompatibility by means of in vitro genetic manipulation.

Budd Hopkins called the hybrids "transgenic beings," which would be a more biologically correct term, if that's the case. "In vitro" in this sense simply means taking place outside of the human body (in a test tube or Petri dish, for example). With a sufficiently advanced genetic technology, there's no reason to assume that aliens couldn't create beings with "hybrid" characteristics via in vitro manipulation of human and alien reproductive material.

To my knowledge, however, no abductee or contactee has reported seeing this actually done in the lab. People have reported seeing the hybrid children at all stages of development.

People have reported having sexual intercourse with other experiencers, and with reptilians, and women have reported becoming pregnant after these sexual encounters.

Women have reported feeling the fetus growing inside them, and seeing it removed after a few weeks or months, to complete development in some sort of artificial womb or incubator. But the actual process of gene splicing and manipulation that we assume must be taking place hasn't been directly observed, as far as I'm aware.

Now perhaps the beings simply feel this aspect of the program is too technical to try to show or explain to the experiencers in detail, or perhaps they are keeping some of the details of this process secret for security reasons. There may, however, be another possibility. Perhaps we *are* reproductively compatible with these beings, even those that look like reptiles.

Are there components of reproduction that we don't yet understand? Things happening on an "energetic" level? Fields of information? Is there some process that is "spiritual" or "inter-dimensional" in nature that allows apparently different species to produce viable offspring?

I'm not saying that this is the case, but I am suggesting that we must keep an open mind and question even the most seemingly well-established biological facts where this phenomenon is concerned. Of course, it could easily be that some unseen technology makes the process possible, or that the genetic alterations are simply being done behind the scenes of the phenomenon.

Reptilians are not "Intrinsically Evil"

In the approximately three decades that UFO researchers have been talking about reptilians, the species has developed an undeserved reputation.

The assumption you hear from some members of the UFO community is that reptilian beings are intrinsically evil. This belief has resulted in a stigma associated with reporting reptilian contact. How did the idea of reptilians as evil entities come about?

The Genesis story, the story of the serpent in the Garden of Eden, who tempted Eve with the fruit of knowledge, may be a part of the explanation. The story could, of course, be interpreted such that the Serpent is actually the good guy; the one who set humanity free from blissful ignorance. Regardless, within Judeo-Christian mythology, the serpent tends to be associated with evil. In the West, you could argue that we are predisposed to think of serpent-like beings as evil.

Historically, people have often turned to religious authorities to help them understand paranormal experiences. Unfortunately, this has sometimes resulted in the entities visiting them being placed in either the category of angels, assumed to be purely good, or demons, assumed to be purely evil.

In ufology it is typically the handsome, human-looking Nordics, sometimes referred to as Pleiadians, who are assumed to be the "angels" and the animal-like reptilians who get labeled as "demons" or negative spiritual beings. Of course, such a black-and-white view is unrealistic.

Human beings are neither purely good, nor purely evil. We are capable of both extremes, but most of the time, as we go about our day-to-day lives, human behavior is more-or-less neutral with regard to such concepts. There's no reason to assume extraterrestrials or inter-dimensional life forms would be any different with regard to their moral and spiritual nature. Nor is there any need to focus on the question of "Are they good guys or bad guys?" to the exclusion of other questions we could be asking about them.

In the mid-nineties, the author David Icke wrote a book called "The Biggest Secret," which posited a sinister global conspiracy led by reptilian humanoids.

In part, Icke's ideas appear to have been a response to his exposure to reports of reptilian contact. It should be noted as well that Barbara Bartholic and Dr. Karla Turner were somewhat negative on reptilians, and this played into the hands of people who came along later wanting to paint the reptilians as villains.

I can't blame people for seeing them in that light, because at the time we had only limited information about the reptilians. In the nineties, most of what was available in the esoteric and UFO literature cast them in a negative light.

I think we had a situation where the initial reports, and the lore that gradually built up around the idea of reptilians, led people to assume that they were "negative" beings, and as a result, people with positive feelings about them were reluctant to speak out, for fear of being told they were being deceived or manipulated by the reptilians, or were merely victims of the Stockholm syndrome: sympathizing with their captors.

Nevertheless, some people were having positive experiences with the reptilians from the beginning. It is interesting to note that there have been cases in which people encountered the reptilians out-of-body or in some other state of being in which they appeared as light beings, and were interpreted as "angels."

It seems that there is something about the reptilian form itself that people have a hard time relating to as anything good or benevolent. Of course, the reptilian appearance is simply a consequence of evolutionary history. Amphibians, mammals, reptiles and birds are just different classes of living beings. Regardless of the origin of one's body, it's the soul inside that's important.

While I was researching this chapter, Nancy wrote to me, "Never at any time did I feel I was being taken against my will, but instead [I was] encouraging his advances. I embraced the feelings we shared and am unable to put them to words. We had done this many times in many lives is what I believe. He is my soulmate."

Many people who have had contact with reptilians can't help but love these beings. Indeed, there have been many cases in which

185

people have felt pure love and acceptance from them. I feel it's important to remind people that there's no shame in loving a reptilian.

Supporting the Experiencers and the Human Future

How can we, as a community, be more supportive of experiencers like Nancy Tremaine, and why should we do so? I think it should go without saying that the people who are reporting these experiences deserve to be treated fairly and with respect, rather than ridiculed or dismissed.

However, many people in our culture still feel that it's okay to poke fun at people who report UFO contact or abduction experiences. In some cases, the people doing this are people in positions of visibility, people whose example others follow. This needs to change if we are to see progress in the way our society deals with the UFO experience.

The late Dr. Carl Sagan was often quoted as saying, "Extraordinary claims require extraordinary evidence." But what does that statement mean, what are its limitations, and how does it apply today, two decades after Dr. Sagan's death? Too often, the quote has been used as a sort of bludgeon by the intolerant to try to get contactees to shut up about their experiences.

What constitutes an extraordinary claim? Further, is the claim of having had a UFO contact experience as "extraordinary" as it once was? In this context, an extraordinary claim is a claim that, if proved true, would revolutionize our understanding of our place in the universe.

Would the claim that one has *had the experience of* meeting a reptilian do that? Would the claim that one has *had the experience of* being taken aboard a UFO or perceived alien craft do that?

No, not at all. It has become clear that many people have had these experiences. This was what they perceived. This is what they remember happening to them. As such, these reports are now something relatively ordinary, rather than extraordinary.

Admittedly, the UFO contact experience sometimes involves various forms of physical or circumstantial evidence that suggest the experience took place, at least in part, at an event-level reality.

In other words, the circumstances surrounding these experiences are *consistent with* the interpretation that they are real, physical events. If one could prove that that interpretation was correct, by means of presenting "extraordinary evidence" in its favor, then *that* would revolutionize our understanding of our place in the universe, as it would mean that "we're not alone."

However, regardless of the large body of circumstantial evidence that exists, no one has yet succeeded in providing the incontrovertible "smoking gun" (i.e., the extraordinary evidence) to prove the validity of the "aliens are here" interpretation.

I think it's fair to infer that no one is likely to do so in the near future. This is simply a limitation we have to accept. It's one of the rules by which the phenomenon operates, and it can guide us as far as what avenues of research, communication and documentation are likely to be most beneficial going forward.

The important distinction I'm making here is that the claim to have *had the experience of* contact is *not* an extraordinary claim. The claim only becomes extraordinary when you assume a particular interpretation of it, and take the experience as a literal representation of events in the physical world.

Of course, many of us do assume such interpretation, but only for pragmatic purposes, rather than for the philosophical purpose of "proving" the reality of alien visitation to skeptics.

I mean, at the pragmatic level, one has to use Occam's razor, and go with the simplest explanation, the notion that the experience is what it appears to be, rather than with an explanation that is needlessly contrived and convoluted. This is simply a matter of living with the experience day-to-day, which is something experiencers have to do, rather than living in denial of it.

So how does this relate to the idea of treating experiencers with fairness and respect? First, it means recognizing that, for the most part, they are not trying to impose their beliefs upon us, nor are they trying to "prove" the reality of UFO contact in a literal sense.

Rather, they are people who have had profound experiences, and they want to share those experiences with someone else, in order to "get it off their chests," or perhaps to share it with society in general, in the hopes of contributing something to collective human knowledge. They are not attempting to be confrontational by sharing the experience, and the rest of us should not be confrontational with them, for example, by incessantly demanding "extraordinary evidence" or proof.

It's better to simply sit with the information, and accept that one doesn't really know the source of the experience. Having a healthy tolerance for uncertainty is helpful when dealing with a phenomenon such as UFO contact.

187

In conclusion, let me simply say that I'm optimistic about the future. Society is moving forward in its treatment of UFO abductees, contactees, and experiencers.

More and more people are waking up to the reality of reptilian contact. In time, cool heads will prevail, and people will see the reptilians as they are, other intelligent beings who have souls just as we have souls.

More of us will remember our contact with these beings, and the overall consequence of this awakening will be uplifting for human civilization. Some of these other beings are people who we can work with, people we're already working with, for our mutual benefit. In coming forward and sharing her story with the world, Nancy Tremaine has contributed her testimony to a growing body of UFO contact literature.

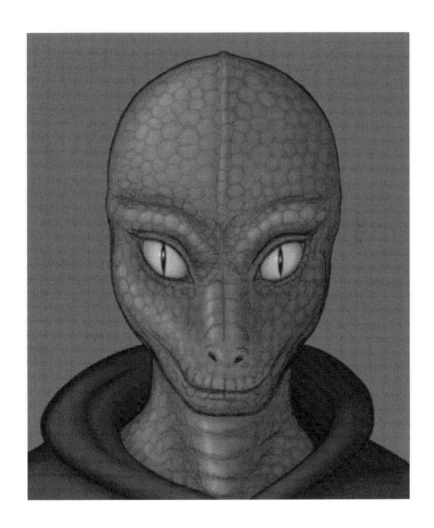

Iyano

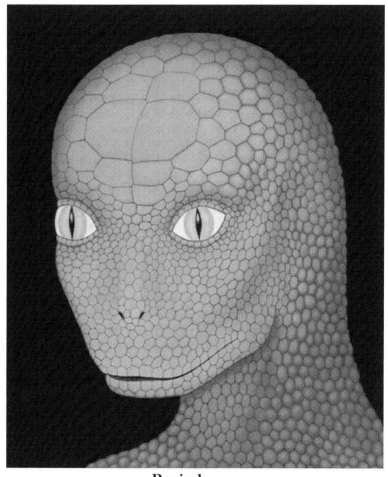

Renjeck

This is an example of a Reptilian without a forehead ridge.

Appendix A
A Primer on Post Traumatic Stress: The Basics

by Michael Austin Melton

For many abductees, the resulting symptom package is referred to as post-traumatic stress disorder. This disorder was initially referred to in the field of ufology/abduction research as "post abduction syndrome" (Hargrove, 2000) when it is seen in alien abductees.

However, it matches so well with post-traumatic stress (PTSD), I am going to refer to post abduction syndrome (PAS) and PTSD as one in the same. If there are any differences, I will be sure to make them clear. Know that for the purposes of understanding this complex collection of symptoms that make up the diagnosis referred to as PTSD/PAS, I am using "*worst case scenario.*" Symptoms and degrees of severity vary from person to person.

The severity of the PTSD/PAS syndrome as a whole depends upon several factors, and here are just a few:

1.   *The Intensity of the Trauma.*   Each person, because of his or her psychological makeup might experience the trauma differently. Included here might be the degree to which they possessed an open mind about the paranormal, or whether or not they were well read in the subject matter. Also consider the level of interaction with the being, if any interaction at all. Intensity can be defined by so many factors. There is not enough room in this book to introduce and explain them all.

2.   *Being Hurt, Losing Something or Someone:* On occasion, the abduction sequence might involve a medical (non-invasive or invasive) procedure. This might involve pain, or an embarrassing sexual procedure. The abductee might be exposed to what the alien refers to as the abductee's hybrid child. Bonding with the hybrid child activates the maternal instinct (and in some cases where men are abducted and exposed to the same, the paternal instinct), and leaving them behind fosters a sense of loss and longing.

3.   *Closeness to the Traumatic Event:* In this case, what level of encounter is experienced? Was it a sighting of an alien craft, the witnessing of aliens at a distance, an actual contact experience with or without abduction? Was it an abduction involving several other people, or seeing other humans on the craft during abduction, or is the person a witness to another individual being abducted?

4.   *Experiencing Loss of Control:* This factor includes not being able to control the panic or anxiety itself resulting in a panic attack, and not being able to predict when or where another abduction will take place. Included here is the knowledge that you cannot escape a future abduction or prevent it from happening if there is the risk of a second or third one. Abductees have been taken from strange and seemingly impossible places. Google that phrase to discover some very strange abductions from very unusual locations.

5.   *Main Determining Factor -- Lack of Support:* This includes alienation from family or friends, and society in general, and includes self-isolation from the now strange and frightening world the experiencer has a difficult time making sense of due to the shattering of their world view. This factor alone makes up a large percentage of the PTSD/PAS syndrome.

The fuel for the PTSD/PAS syndrome is the attempt at reassembling the person's worldview. For the experiencer, the world around them has taken on a new meaning as they question the meaning of their life, reassessing the people they love, how the world works, their faith, as well as themselves. The person might ask repeatedly, "What's going on here?" or, "Why is the world so different and strange to me now?"

The Ingredients of PTSD/PAS:

Post-Traumatic Stress Disorder ("PTSD") is a collection of symptoms. Many of these symptoms could very well stand on their own as disorders. The severity of PTSD depends upon the individual's constitution, or their susceptibility to the particular symptoms included under the heading of PTSD/PAS. Overall however, the following symptoms are found in everyone who suffers from PTSD, regardless of cause, ranging from involvement in military conflict, being in or being a witness to a catastrophe, or having been abducted by aliens:

1. *Fear and Anxiety Caused by Anything that Reminds the Person of the Trauma:* A good example of this would be seeing the cover of Whitley Strieber's book "Communion." Experiencers and some non-experiencers likely had a startle reaction to that cover. Another example might be a person suddenly hearing electromechanical noises or sounds, such as a beeping noise, or seeing motion outside a window, experiencing certain odors, or colors. Certain television shows or movies might cause an attack of uncontrollable anxiety.

2. *Nightmares, Vivid Memories or Dreams that Cause the Person to feel as if the traumatic event is happening again:* This particular factor is much more accentuated in people who are "multiple abductees." Vivid dreams and images are hard to distinguish from the actual event.

3. *Pervasive Sense of Isolation from Others:* This includes feeling ostracized, lonely and feeling alone even in a room full of people, and isolated from family and friends. This also includes feelings that the person does not belong in society anymore, or that they do not belong on this planet with other humans.

4. *Feeling emotionally numb, and having no desire to engage in things that used to be interesting:* This includes little or no emotional response to sad or happy situations, not being able to laugh at a favorite comedian's material, not engaging in fun or exciting activities the person used to enjoy, and feeling affectively dissociated from significant others.

5. *The Onset or Worsening of Depression:* As the person tries to rebuild their worldview and find the task daunting, depression in many cases becomes an able adversary in the process. The person's sense of hopelessness grows deeper as they begin questioning the reality of the current "status quo." This can be suppressed somewhat if the person has social support of some kind.

6. *A Constant Sense of Being in Danger:* The person remains vigilant in their environment – always keeping an eye out for anything related to the trauma that might be harmful or threatening. This might also operate on a sub-

conscious level as well. For example once again, if a person walks into a bookstore and happens to glance at Strieber's "Communion" book cover, and recoils, that would be the fear and vigilance in operation. The person might be jittery, and irritable or "snappy" toward others

7.   *Pervasive Feeling that Something Bad is About to Happen:* This symptom would likely be worse in people who have been abducted in the daylight, from their automobile (there are a few cases of this happening while the person is driving!), at various times, or in various locations. Some abductees can sense when an abduction is about to take place by way of a beeping or ringing in the ears, and any sound that mimics this stimulus can cause panic.

8.   *Difficulty Sleeping or Staying Asleep:* Out of twelve types of sleep disorders, two fit this category well. "Adjustment insomnia" occurs when the person is introduced to a new array of stressors (realization of being abducted, or actually being abducted). The mind and body, in the process of adjustment, suffers this kind of insomnia. "Psychophysiological insomnia" results from excessive worry. At night when it is time for bed, the person might decide to keep the lights on, keep the television or radio on, or engage in reading or playing Solitaire. The excessive worry, not the action or activity, is at the root of this form of insomnia. Regardless of the worry and the attempts to avoid abduction, the alien abductors usually get their way.

9.   *During the Day, the Person Usually has Difficulty Concentrating:* This is caused by intrusive thoughts, of course the anxiety, feeling on the edge of losing control, and worrying about the world around them. This inability to stay focused usually interferes with accomplishing the activities of daily living.

There are other symptoms too, such as the *inability to get along with family members* for obvious reasons in the case of abduction. The person might *avoid the place(s) where the abduction took place.* The person might choose to sleep in a different bedroom or on a living room couch in order to avoid detection.

They might pull away from society, friends and family and self-isolate. Feeling like they do not belong, or are different than

194

others, or they have a fear of ridicule or rejection, it is easier for the abductee to turn into a hermit than to deal with the additional stress.

Individuals who carry the burden of a severe mental disorder such as a deep depression might fall into a pattern of substance abuse. At the very worst, the person might have suicidal ideation with or without a plan to kill themselves, or the person might actually try to kill themselves, and sadly, some are successful in this course of action.

I must place a disclaimer here. In the course of *my* work with abductees, I have not yet worked with anyone who resorted to suicidal attempts or who expressed ideation. I am not saying there has never been a case where the abductee killed himself or herself. There might be a number of cases like that.

However, I have never encountered an actively suicidal abductee. Many of the abductees I've worked with suffer with *some* symptoms, but not *all* of the symptoms at once. Each symptom, as I said earlier, varies in intensity from person to person. Each symptom can stand on its own as a disorder. As they work toward successful integration of their new reality into their worldview, and all the "pieces of the puzzle fit nicely together," symptoms begin to fade, but never fully disperse.

Nancy Tremaine is a great example of someone who has successfully worked through most of her issues and created a new worldview. She has integrated her abductions and involvement with the reptilians so well; she is working with them in an effort to help each species develop an understanding and a relationship built upon cooperation and sharing. She continues to this day with the process of integration. It is an excellent example of a process referred to as "*Symbiosis.*"

How can the average person help an experiencer who appears to have symptoms of PTSD? The most important curative factor is to have *a good set of ears* and *a willingness to listen.*

When an experiencer talks to someone who really "hears" their story, and who accepts them at face value, unconditionally, the battle in which the experiencer is engaged in with life has been won by at least fifty percent. The rest of the job should be left to a professional. These sympathetic professionals who work with experiencers can be found in the files of several organizations. You might suggest the experiencer contact one of the following organizations:

1) *Starborn Support International*: This organization specializes in "case management" and support for people who are experiencers. There are support groups in several states, and more

states will be jumping aboard as time progresses. The link to services is http://www.starbornsupport.org/services/, and there the experiencer can find the pathways to help and assistance.

Founder and Chairman Audrey Hewins is open to contact directly. You can send her an email at "aah3273@yahoo.com" (without the quotes). She will refer you to someone in the organization who is trained to listen and support experiencers. You might even talk to me!

2) *The Foundation for Research into Extraterrestrial Experiences (FREE):* Rey Hernandez and his esteemed co-chairs and board members have created a unique program called "The Buddy System." When you contact FREE at http://www.experiencer.org/, you can find all of the contact information. When an experiencer contacts FREE, they are paired with another experiencer with a similar story and background for the purposes of mutual support. This system is quite effective.

If there are problems that extend beyond that of the experiencer, such as mental illness or a case of PTSD so severe it is crippling to the individual, then you can have either organization locate sympathetic professionals -- psychologists, psychiatrists, physicians, counselors, and social workers who are willing to work with the experiencer.

CORONARY VASCULATURE

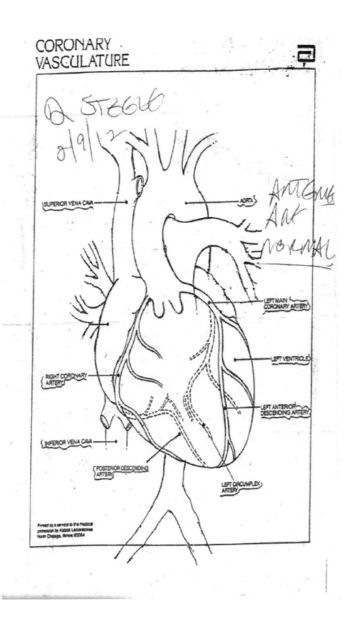

Patient Name:	TREMAINE
MRN:	
Date of Birth:	10/04/1949
Admit Date:	02/08/2012
Discharge Date:	02/09/2012
Account Number:	
Patient Type:	Inpatient
Attending:	Ibrahim MD, Ragheda

Consultation

Consult

Date : 02/09/2012 9:11:11 AM EST

Electronically Signed By: Vedala MD, Giridhar   Date Signed: 02/09/2012 9:11:11 AM EST

Systolic BP   91/59 (02/09 07:51) 138/72 (02/08 18:00)
Diastolic BP   91/59 (02/09 07:51) 138/72 (02/08 18:00)

General
Exam: Alert and oriented x3, vital signs stable.
Eye
Eye: conjunctiva clear.
HENT/Mouth
Head: normocephalic, atraumatic.
Throat: no erythema.
Mouth: mucosal lining pink and moist without lesions.
Neck
Exam: no lymphadenopathy, no thyromegaly, no carotid bruits.
Respiratory
Lungs: clear to auscultation.
Cardiovascular
Exam: Regular rate and rhythm, no murmur, no lower extremity edema.
Gastrointestinal
Exam: bowel sounds present, abdomen soft, non tender.
Musculoskeletal
Head: symmetric appearance.
Hands/Wrists: hands grossly normal.
Legs/Knees: legs grossly normal.
Integumentary
Exam: no rashes.
Neurologic
Exam: Alert & oriented x 3.
Psychiatric
Alert.
Appropriate.

Results Review
General Results
Lab Results : LAB
Lab Results : LAB
2/9/2012 4:42 EST

Sodium Level	139 mEq/L
Potassium Level	4.0 mEq/L
Chloride Level	103 mEq/L
Carbon Dioxide Level	30 mEq/L

Printed Date: 02/14/13
Printed Time: 15:32

St. Joseph Mercy Hospital, Ann Arbor
St. Joseph Mercy Hospital – Ann Arbor

Ypsilanti, Michigan

A Member of Trinity Health
Livonia, Michigan

Patient Name: TREMAINE
MRN:
Date of Birth: 10/04/1949
Admit Date: 02/08/2012
Discharge Date: 02/09/2012
Account Number:
Patient Type: Inpatient
Attending: Ibrahim MD, Ragheda

Discharge Summary

Discharge Summary/HWDD (TH)

Date: 02/10/2012 5:32:38 AM EST

Electronically Signed By: Ibrahim MD, Ragheda   Date Signed: 02/10/2012 5:32:38 AM EST

had nonspecific T wave changes in the anteroseptal leads. Troponins were abnormal and peaked at 2.89. She's had no recurrence of symptoms. She was given some nitroglycerin and morphine which improved her symptoms. placed on iv heparin, ASA, beta blocker

hospital course
NSTEMI

cardiology was consultedpt, pt underwent heat cath through Right arm that showed nl coronory arteries but WMA with anteriolateral akinesis and small focal area, so probably she had spasm, wanted to start CCB, and observe pt over night as her BP is running on low side,but pt insisted on leaving, on time of discharge pt didn't have any more episodes of CP , no SOB, felt okay, vitals remained stable,and she will be discharged on small dose ccb with norvasc 2.5 mg qd,and to f/u with cardiology dr vedala in 5–7 days

Discharge Procedures
Discharge Procedures: heart catheterziation.
Discharged Lab Results
Selected Lab Results

Lab	Collected On
Hemoglobin	12.6 gm/dL 02/09/12 05:00
Hematocrit	36.5 % 02/09/12 05:00
WBC Count	5.6 thou/mcL 02/09/12 05:00
Platelet Count	258 thou/mcL 02/09/12 05:00
Sodium Level	139 mEq/L 02/09/12 05:00
Potassium Level	4.0 mEq/L 02/09/12 05:00
Creatinine	1.01 mg/dL 02/09/12 05:00
BUN	14 mg/dL 02/09/12 05:00
Glucose Level	H 121 mg/dL 02/09/12 05:00

Discharge Medications
MEDICATIONS

This is your new list of medications. Keep it with you at all times. Your doctor may have changed doses, added, held or stopped some of your medications. Ask your doctor if you have any questions.

NEW MEDICATIONS YOU WILL BE TAKING AT HOME WITH INSTRUCTIONS ON HOW AND WHEN TO TAKE FOR EACH MEDICATION.

AmLODIPine (Norvasc 2.5 mg oral tablet)
1 Tab = 2.5 mg By Mouth once a day

MEDICATION(S) YOU TOOK AT HOME PRIOR TO YOUR VISIT. PLEASE CHECK THE INSTRUCTIONS, THEY MAY HAVE CHANGED.

ALPRAZolam (Xanax)
By Mouth once a day

BuPROPion (Wellbutrin)
By Mouth

Printed Date: 02/14/13
Printed Time: 15:32

199

St. Joseph Mercy Hospital, Ann Arbor
St. Joseph Mercy Hospital – Ann Arbor

Ypsilanti, Michigan

A Member of Trinity Health
Livonia, Michigan

Patient Name: TREMAINE
MRN:
Date of Birth: 10/04/1949
Admit Date: 09/04/2012
Discharge Date: 09/08/2012
Account Number:
Patient Type: Inpatient
Attending: Trifunovic MD, Borivoje M

MRI

1   Other-

Exam Name:	Accession Number:	Ordering Physician:	Exam Date/Time:
MRI Brain w and w/o Contrast	MR-12-0060772	Obi MD, Kenneth O	09/05/2012 9:00:00 PM EDT

FINAL REPORT

Report

BRAIN MRI
NECK MRA

INDICATION: Neurologic deficit. Ataxia. CVA. Cerebrovascular disease.

TECHNIQUE: Multiplanar, multisequential images of the brain were performed with and without 10 mL Gadavist contrast. 2D and 3D time-of-flight unenhanced images performed. Following the administration of 10 mL Gadavist contrast, images of the extracranial neck vessels were performed with multiplanar reformations.

COMPARISON: Head CT 09/04/2012. Carotid ultrasound 09/05/2012.

FINDINGS:

BRAIN MRI: No evidence of acute infarction. No evidence of acute parenchymal hemorrhage. No midline shift or hydrocephalus. No expansile or enhancing mass. Nonspecific white matter change suggestive of minimal chronic microangiopathy. No significant global volume loss. No pathologic extraaxial collection. Major expected intracranial central vascular flow voids are present.

NECK MRA: Three-vessel aortic arch. Origins of the common carotid arteries are patent. Atherosclerotic disease of the carotid bifurcations result in less than 25% stenosis of the proximal ICAs bilaterally, according to NASCET criteria. Origins of the vertebral arteries are patent. The left vertebral artery is mildly dominant. The vertebral arteries demonstrate antegrade flow bilaterally.

IMPRESSION:
1. No acute infarction or intracranial mass.
2. No significant stenosis in the extracranial circulation.

Reading Location: AASJPRW2012
~~~~~~~~ FINAL REPORT ~~~~~~~~
Dictated By: Kaakaji MD, Rami 09/05/2012 22:11
Assigned Physician: Kaakaji MD, Rami
Reviewed and Electronically Signed By: Kaakaji MD, Rami 09/05/2012 23:05
Transcribed by: UD 09/05/2012 22:18
Technologist: LB8,MS

Printed Date: 02/15/13
Printed Time: 13:28

Rendering Provider: Garwood, Mark D MD   Phone: (810)229-9799
Practice: Greater Ann Arbor Neurology Associates
Address: 2300 Genoa Business Park Dr, Suite 190, BRIGHTON, MI48114   Phone: (810)229-9799

Visit Date: Monday, December 03, 2012

Patient: Tremaine,
416 North Ann, Fowlerville, MI48836
Medical Record #: 89070   DOB: October 04, 1949   Sex: Female
home: (517)294-9637
Status: Complete.
Visit Last Saved: 12/04/2012 09:35 PM.

CC / HPI:
PCP: Dr. James Alford:

Dear Dr. Alford. Your patient presented to our Brighton office for an EEG to further evaluate recent syncopal episodes.

Current Medication:
alprazolam 0.5 mg tablet, 1 Tablet(s), PO and TID.
Aspir-81 81 mg tablet,delayed release.
Prempro 0.3 mg-1.5 mg tablet.
bupropion HCl SR 100 mg tablet,sustained-release.

Dx:

780.2 SYNCOPE AND COLLAPSE

Services Performed:

(95819) EEG- Standard/ Sleep Deprived

Plan Note:
Technique: This was a 19 channel EEG performed with one additional channel of EKG monitoring using standard international 10-20 electrode placement and bipolar, transverse, and referential montages.

Interpretation: The patient's waking background posterior rhythm was symmetric 10.5 Hz alpha with an amplitude of approximately 40 microvolts. Photic stimulation resulted in a symmetric occipital driving effect. Hyperventilation resulted in no abnormalities in background activity. No focal, lateralized, or epileptiform findings were seen. This EEG occurred during wakefulness. EKG showed NSR.

Impression: This was a normal EEG during wakefulness.

Sincerely,

Mark D Garwood

201

Made in United States
Troutdale, OR
06/04/2023

10439315R00116